Typing and Word Processing Dictionary

Typing and Word Processing Dictionary

Joyce Stananought and Derek Stananought are well-known as writers and lecturers both in this country and overseas, and are both experienced teachers and examiners. Joyce was formerly Principal Lecturer and Deputy Head of Department of Business Information Processing at Salford College of Technology. Derek was formerly Senior Lecturer at Manchester Polytechnic. Other Chambers titles include *Typewriting Theory and Practice* and *Advanced Typewriting Theory and Practice* by Joyce Stananought, and *Keyboarding* byDerek Stananought.

Typing and Word Processing Dictionary

Joyce Stananought BEd(Hons)

Derek Stananought BEd(Hons)

Chambers

Published by W & R Chambers Ltd,
43-45 Annandale Street, Edinburgh EH7 4AZ

British Library Cataloguing in Publication Data
Stananought, Joyce
Typing and word processing dictionary.
1. Typing – Encyclopaedias 2. Word processing – Encyclopaedias
I. Title II. Stananought, Derek
652.3'003'21

ISBN 0-550-18077-X

Acknowledgements
The authors express their thanks to Chambers Publishers and Sanda Press for the illustrations used in this book.

Cover design by William Ross Design
Typeset by Impact Repro, Edinburgh
Printed in Great Britain at the University Press, Cambridge

Preface

The ever-increasing developments in word processing technology have led to the introduction of many new words and terms and some changes in document layout. Chambers *Typing and Word Processing Dictionary* provides a comprehensive reference source for today's office worker.

The term 'jargon' is often applied to the specialist terms used in word processing to describe the hardware, software, functions and working. The authors are experts in their fields, and they have designed this handy book to help typists and word processor operators to understand these specialist terms by providing straightforward, jargon-free explanations. In addition, layout guides are also included to illustrate up-to-date forms of document layout.

Chambers *Typing and Word Processing Dictionary* is suitable for the syllabuses of all the public examination boards covering the areas of typing, word processing and office technology. It deals with the most common words, terms and layouts used in examinations and in the modern office. It will also serve as an ideal reference text for those returning to the office environment and wishing to refresh or up-date their knowledge.

A

abbreviations A list of abbreviations and their meanings is provided in an appendix at the back of this book.

It is not possible to set out definite 'rules' for knowing when to leave words in their abbreviated form and when to type them in full. A great deal depends on the author's preference or the general practice followed in an organisation.

Some words may be typed either in their abbreviated form or in full, depending on the context, eg, *Dept* (Department), *No* (Number), *Ref* (Reference), *Tel* (Telephone). When they form part of a company name, *Ltd, Bros, Inc, Co, PLC* or *&* are acceptable in their abbreviated form. The ampersand (*&*) and words such as *company* and *limited* should be typed in full in continuous text. Abbreviations such as *Ave, Rd, St, Cresc,* days of the week and months of the year, should be typed in full. As a general rule *eg, etc, ie* and *NB* are acceptable in their abbreviated form.

Abbreviated words are often used as headings in tables because of the need to save space. In manuscript drafts, some people use the initial letter of a word followed by a long dash to indicate that the word(s) should be written in full, eg, *The P— M—will be at the H— of C— tomorrow.* (The Prime Minister will be at the House of Commons tomorrow.)

When open punctuation style is used, you should omit full stops from abbreviations.

abbreviations file A special facility on a word processor used to store fairly small amounts of text that are frequently used, such as difficult technical or medical terms. The text is keyed into the file together with an abbreviation and coded identifiers, such as *ps* for *psychasthenia*. These items are stored on disk and when necessary they may be recalled and inserted in a document simply by keying in the coded symbol. The abbreviations file may also be known as the glossary, vocabulary list or lexicon.

accents An accent is a symbol placed above or below a character to indicate the way in which a word should be pronounced, eg, pâté, garçon, Noël. They are used more extensively in foreign languages than in English. The accents may be provided on the keyboard character set as dead keys. In this case the accent key is typed first, but the typing mechanism does not move on until the character the accent belongs to is typed.

Alternatively, special accented character keys may be fitted to the machine, or interchangeable print wheels containing accented characters may be fitted. If your machine does not have the facility to type accents, insert them neatly in ink on the completed copy.

access To gain entry to information stored on a disk so that it can be read, amended and/or printed.

access time The time taken to retrieve a document stored on a disk.

accuracy Typewriting accuracy refers to the correctness of a completed document. The emphasis is not simply on typing without any errors, but also on identifying and correcting any errors that may be noticed while you are typing or when you proofread the document. An accurate document is one which is a true transcript of the original and which contains no errors of any kind.

acoustic cover (acoustic hood) A cover or hood for a printer that reduces the noise made during the printing process.

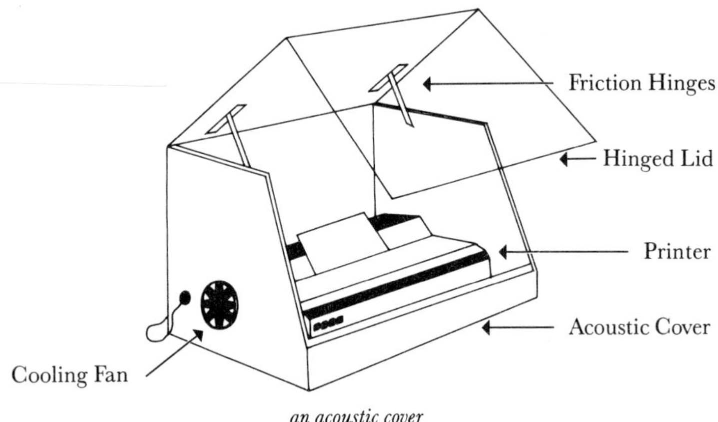

an acoustic cover

acronyms Artificial words made from the initial letters of the name of an organisation, etc, are known as *acronyms*. These should be typed without any full stops, eg, NATO, UNICEF.

addendum (plural addenda) There are two types of addendum: (*a*) explanatory notes that accompany a document, such as a report, or are included in a book; and (*b*) notes alerting the reader to omissions or errors to be found in the work. An explanatory addendum is generally placed at the end of the work, whilst an omissions addendum may be placed in a noticeable position at the beginning of the work.

addressee The person to whom a letter is addressed (the recipient).

addresses in business letters Two addresses are normally found on a business letter—the sender's and the recipient's. The sender's address is generally printed at the top of the page. The recipient's address (or addressee's address) is normally typed between the date and the salutation on the left-hand side of the page. An alternative position for the recipient's address is at the foot of the page, below the sender's signature and designation. (See **letters.**)

addresses on envelopes or labels The destination to which a letter is to be despatched may be typed on an envelope or a self-adhesive label. The position of the address differs between the two but there are presentational details which are standard.

On an envelope the address is typed parallel to the longest edge of the envelope. Start the first line at least one third of the way down the envelope to allow space for the stamps and ensure that the postal franking does not obliterate the address. Type the address fairly centrally across the width of the envelope.

When self-adhesive labels are used, start the address at least one line space below the top edge of the label and finish it at least one space above the bottom edge. This generally means typing the address on no more than six line spaces. Start the address at least 5 mm from the left-hand edge of the label.

With both envelopes and labels, start each line of the address on a separate line wherever possible. If it is necessary to type the postcode on the same line as the last item of the address, leave two character spaces between the items. Use blocked layout, open punctuation style and single line spacing.

Mr B L Garstang Chief Accountant Garsdale Printers Ltd 47 Woodland Way Preston PR3 4AJ	Mrs V M Caddick Accounts Department Trysdale Products Ltd Trysdale House 57 Oakdale Avenue Leeds LS3 9RK	Mr A Jasindra Chief Accountant Bel-Oba Textyles Ltd 92 Carterwood Road Birmingham B6 7PP
Miss R Turton Chief Accountant EGA Engineering Ltd 22 Arnadale Crescent Bristol BS3 4JJ	Mr K Litchfield Accounts Department Fiddler Fresh Foods 42 Larchfield Lane Wiffenbury Plymouth PL7 9WB	Mrs B Western-Jones Accounts Department Danvers & Rowe Ltd 71 South Main Street Lancaster LA1 OED

address on labels

agenda A document consisting of a list of numbered items to be discussed at a meeting, and the order in which they will be taken, which is drawn up by the Secretary in consultation with the Chairperson. The agenda is sent to each person entitled to attend, generally in advance of the meeting to allow members time to prepare for discussion of the items. Certain standard items appear on the majority of agendas, such as apologies for absence, minutes of the last meeting, matters arising from the minutes of the last meeting, correspondence, the date of the next meeting and any other business. Other agenda items concerned with a particular meeting will include relevant matters raised by the Chairperson and Secretary, or by other members of the committee or organisation for which the meeting is held.

Use the blocked style of layout for both versions and type the agenda items in single line spacing with at least one clear line space between the items. If possible, leave additional line spacing between items to allow room for members to make notes. A more detailed copy of the agenda may be produced for the Chairperson containing additional notes to help in the efficient conduct of the meeting and this is often set out with all the agenda items typed on the left-hand side of the page, leaving the right-hand side clear for note-making.

CORFIELD DISTRICT TWINNING ASSOCIATION

A N N U A L   G E N E R A L   M E E T I N G

TO BE HELD IN THE CONFERENCE ROOM
AT THE CORFIELD DISTRICT OFFICES
75 TRENSHAM STREET, CORFIELD
ON MONDAY, 27 OCTOBER 199- AT 7.30 PM

A G E N D A

1 Apologies for absence.

2 Minutes of the Annual General Meeting held on Monday, 19 October 199- (Appendix A, attached).

3 Matters arising from the minutes of the last Annual General Meeting.

4 Chairman's Report.

5 Secretary's Report.

6 Treasurer's Report.

7 Election of Officers: Chairman, Vice-Chairman, Treasurer and Secretary (see Appendix B, attached).

8 Election of Committee.

9 Activities and events in the coming year (see Appendix C, attached).

10 Any other business.

11 Date of the next Annual General Meeting.

an agenda

aligning paper Insert the paper into your typewriter or printer in such a way that the line of text, when printed, will be parallel with the top and bottom edges of the paper. Use the alignment scale on the typewriter, or turn the paper forward and ensure that the left and right sides of the paper, or the top and bottom edges, are precisely edge-to-edge.

alignment Horizontal alignment refers to the position of printed characters along the line. When you type items against pre-printed headings, such as *To, From, Date* and *Ref* on a memorandum form, use the platen knob or interliner on your typewriter to adjust the alignment so that the typed characters are precisely aligned with the printed headings.

Vertical alignment refers to the position of numbers or text below each other, as in a table containing several columns. Items starting at the same scale position are referred to as *left aligned.* A column of numbers is usually typed so that all the figures end at the same point, and these are referred to as *right aligned.* Numbers containing a decimal point are usually aligned on the decimal point (*decimal alignment*).

alignment scale A plastic or metal scale indicator found either side of the typing point on a typewriter. The line of text should rest on the alignment indicator, which may be a line printed on a plastic scale or the top edge of a metal scale. Vertical marks on the scale point to the middle of a typed character. Use this scale to ensure precise alignment of type against pre-printed headings, or when re-inserting a document into the typewriter to correct an error.

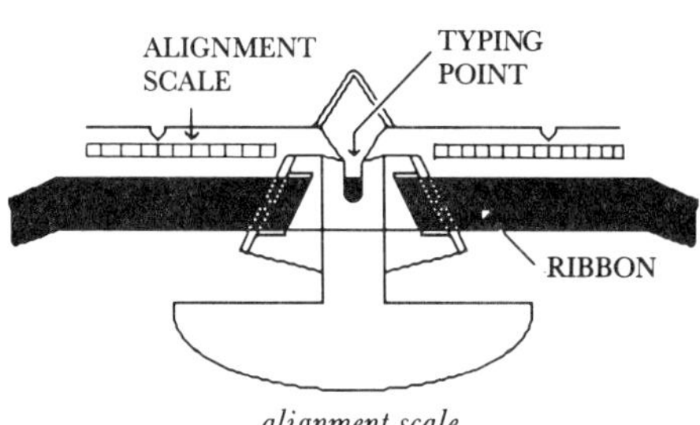

alignment scale

alphabetical order Items sorted into alphabetical order are listed according to the position in the alphabet of the initial character. Sorting may be carried out in ascending alphabetical order (from A to Z) or descending order (from Z to A). When more than one item starts with the same character, the sort takes place on the second and then the third characters, and so on, eg, *Aaron, Abbey, Acland, Acton, Actyll, Adams.*

Before typing, sort items into alphabetical order and write a number against each one to indicate the order in which it should be typed. Check the list before typing to ensure that no mistakes have been made, and check the completed list to ensure that it contains the correct number of items. On a word processor you can key in the items without pre-sorting, and simply type them in the correct order by positioning the cursor appropriately. Some word processors can automatically sort a list of items into asecending or descending alphabetical order.

alphanumeric Any combination of letters of the alphabet and numbers, eg DC44706A or 9904 XXA2.

ampersand The symbol & which represents the word *and.* The ampersand may be used when it forms part of a business name, as part of a married couple's name, in addresses or when normal usage places it within an abbreviation, eg, Patel & Armstrong, Mr & Mrs Johnson, 15 & 17 Deyes Lane, E&OE, O&M. In all other cases the ampersand should always be typed in full as *and.*

anti-glare screen A removable screen that can be attached to the VDU in front of the existing screen to prevent glare reflecting off the screen from lighting or bright sunlight. Anti-glare screens are also said to enhance the text display, making it easier to read, and to reduce the problems caused by static. They may also be referred to as anti-static screens.

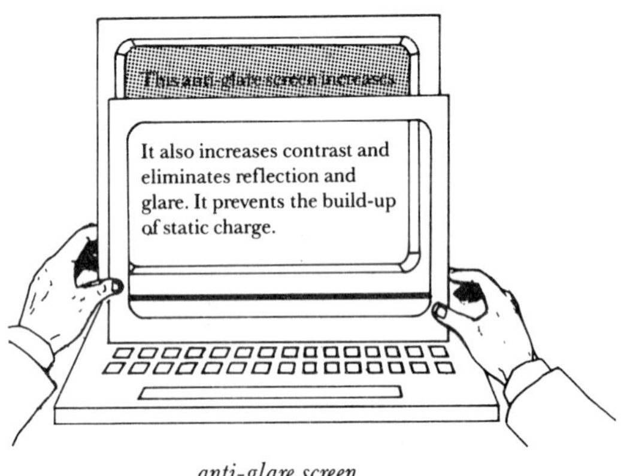

anti-glare screen

apostrophe The single quotation mark (') is used for the apostrophe.

appendix Information or explanatory notes relating to a book, or a document such as a report, which is kept separate from the main text, eg, tables of figures, lists of addresses, graphs or charts. An appendix (plural *appendices*) is always found at the end of the book or document.

applications program Any computer program designed to carry out a particular function (or application) such as word processing, accounting, producing spreadsheets, databases, presentation graphics, communications, etc, or a combination of these applications. Such a program may also be referred to as an *applications package*, and a combination of several programs is known as an *integrated package.*

arabic numbers These are the normal, everyday numbers 1,2,3,4, etc. These are also known as *cardinal numbers.*

archival storage The storage of disks and documents, that are infrequently required for reference purposes, in a safe place as back-up copies, or until they are destroyed.

arithmetic function Some word processors allow the automatic addition, subtraction, multiplication and division of figures displayed in the columns and rows of a table. This function is useful for checking whether the figures you have typed are correct by comparing the totals produced by the computer with those on the original document.

ascender The part of the lower-case characters *b,d,h,k* and *l* that extends above the line of type.

attention note on a letter and envelope Some organisations prefer mail to be addressed 'for the attention of' a particular person, rather than to individuals. This means that all letters can be opened in the mail department and sent to the appropriate department for attention, even if the individual has left the firm or is on holiday. Where an attention note is used, the correct salutation is 'Dear Sirs.'

Type the attention note at the left margin of the letter, between the date and the recipient's address, or between the recipient's address and the salutation, with at least one clear line space above and below it. Use lower-case characters with initial capitals and underline, or all capitals, eg, FOR THE ATTENTION OF MS B M SINCLAIR. Some people abbreviate this to FAO MS B M SINCLAIR. Remember to include the attention note on the envelope. Type it as the first item of the address details, with a clear line space before the start of the address.

audio-typing Audio-typing, or audio-transcription, consists of typing direct from dictated messages recorded on magnetic tape on a specialised business tape-recorder. The typist listens to the dictated text through ear-phones and controls the speed at which the tape travels by means of a foot pedal to allow continuous typing. Transcription machines offer many facilities, including length of dictation indicators, stop, start, reverse and forward wind.

author The term used in typewriting and word processing to refer to the originator, or writer, of a document.

automatic functions and operations All functions and operations on a word processor (and many functions on an electronic typewriter) are carried out automatically in response to commands entered from the keyboard or by means of the mouse. Explanations of the various automatic functions and operations will be found under their actual names in this book.

B

background printing The facility offered by some word processors for the operator to continue working on a document on the screen (in the foreground) while printing is taking place (ie in the background). The system automatically makes a temporary copy of the document to be printed and prints from that copy. This allows the operator to work much more speedily and efficiently.

backing sheet A sheet of paper used behind the typing sheet, intended to prolong the life of the roller on a typewriter. Rollers are now made of strong materials and backing sheets are not really necessary on modern machines. Where continuous stationery is used on a word processor printer it is not possible to use a backing sheet.

backspace The operation of reversing movement from right to left across a line of type on a typewriter or on a VDU screen. The backspace key is used for this purpose on a typewriter, and the left cursor key on a word processor. Note that the backspace key on a word processor keyboard is used for backspace deletion of text. The backspace key is generally located at the top right-hand corner of the QWERTY keyboard, labelled with a left-pointing arrow.

backspace delete key (See **delete text**.)

back-up copy On some word processing systems a back-up copy of each document is automatically taken by the system, and stored and listed on the directory or index. The back-up copy may be listed with an indicator such as BAK, as shown in the example directory listing below.

```
MEMO      MEMO.BAK      REPORT     REPORT.BAK
LETTER    LETTER.BAK    AGENDA     AGENDA.BAK
PRICES    PRICES.BAK    CLIENTS    CLIENTS.BAK
```

Whenever a document is recalled to the screen and edited, the revised version is stored under the document name, and the previous version is transferred to the back-up copy file. The version that was in the back-up copy file is deleted. In this way there is always a copy of the document as it existed before the latest series of editing changes were made.

back-up disk A copy of any disk, such as the applications disk (if permitted under the copyright of that disk) or any disk containing your stored date (the working disk), taken for security reasons. Disks can become damaged or corrupted during use, sometimes due to a machine fault. New applications disks can be obtained from your supplier, but a delay is inevitable and in some cases costly. Work stored on your working disk could be totally lost if a back-up copy is not available, or it could take days or weeks to re-type your work from hard copy. A back-up disk is also referred to as a *security copy* or an *archive disk*.

backward feed The technique used if you wish to make a correction on a sheet of paper that is stapled at the top to other sheets, without undoing the staple. Put a spare sheet of paper into the typewriter and press the return key several times. Insert the bottom edge of the page to be corrected behind this extra sheet and roll the paper down until the spare sheet can be removed. Ensure that the line of type is accurately aligned before making the correction.

ballooned words An editing mark, or correction sign, encircling information to be inserted into the text at the point indicated by the end of the 'string' of the balloon.

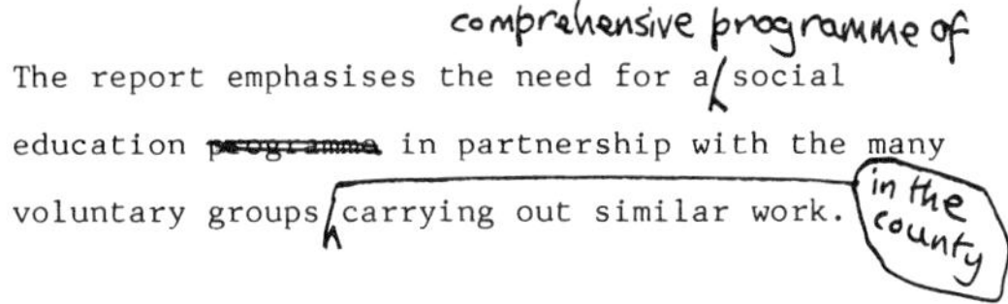
comprehensive programme of
The report emphasises the need for a social
education programme in partnership with the many
voluntary groups carrying out similar work.
in the county

A number of detailed area profiles have been drawn
up which give a clear picture of existing services
the areas
in each area and also identify where further work
is needed.
and, for the first time, these

CORRECTED VERSION

The report emphasises the need for a comprehensive programme of social education in partnership with the many voluntary groups in the county carrying out similar work.

A number of detailed area profiles have been drawn up and, for the first time, these give a clear picture of existing services in each area and identify the areas where further work is needed.

ballooned words

bell zone On typewriters with a manual carriage return, a warning bell rings eight to twelve character spaces from the right margin stop to warn you of the approach of the end of the line. The number of spaces varies from machine to machine. The area between the sound of the bell and the right margin stop is known as the bell zone.

On word processors and electronic typewriters with an automatic carriage return the bell is replaced with an automatic command to the system to indicate the approach of the end of the line, and the space between this command and the right margin stop is known as the *hot zone*. (See **hot zone**.)

bibliography A list of books, reports or articles related to information contained in a document. The bibliography is usually typed at the end of a section or chapter of the book or report, or at the end of the document.

bi-directional printing A bi-directional printer carries out the printing operation in two directions, from left to right and then right to left. This speeds up the printing process. A machine that prints only from left to right is known as a *uni-directional* printer.

blind carbon copy (bcc) One or more additional copies may be taken of a letter or other document and sent to an individual or a number of people who have an interest in the topic. If the sender of the letter does not wish the recipient to know that these copies have been sent, the initials BCC (or bcc), followed by the names of the people receiving them are typed on the carbon copies only. If photocopies of the document are used instead of carbon copies, these details are omitted from the top copy and typed on the master used to produce the photocopies.

block A section of text, from a single line to several screen pages, which the word processor considers and manipulates as a single entity when carrying out such operations as cut, copy, delete, save or embolden. The block is identified, or marked, by placing a coded symbol at the start and end of the block, or by highlighting it in reverse video.

This is an example of 'marking' a block of text so that it may be deleted, moved, centred, emboldened and so on.

The section or block of text is identified by placing a coded symbol at the start and end of the text or highlighted by placing it in reverse video. This has been placed in reverse video.

You give the word processor an instruction to carry out any of the above functions, upon which the text will be deleted, centred, etc.

'marking' a block of text

block centring When several items are to be block centred, the longest line of text is centred on the page. The first character of this line becomes the left margin for the remaining items which all start at this position.

TERRERLEAN HOTELS

Breaks and Family Holidays

We have hotels in over twenty-five locations from Aviemore in the north to Weymouth in the south. All our hotels offer:

TOURING TRIPS
FAMILY HOLIDAYS
SENIOR CITIZEN BREAKS
WEEKEND AND MIDWEEK BREAKS

All hotels have extensive leisure facilities, including indoor pools, tennis courts, children's activities and full entertainment programmes.

block centring

blocked style The form of typewriting layout in which all lines of text paragraphs start at the left margin. These are known as blocked paragraphs. When the blocked style is used, headings may be blocked or centred, and tables or sub-paragraphs may be inset from the left and right margin.

boilerplating A word processing operation in which sections of various documents stored on disk are automatically combined to form a new document. This is a very quick, time-saving way of producing a new document such as a letter from standard paragraphs that have previously been keyed in and stored on disk. Because the stored text has already been proofread and checked, the completed document needs less checking. The operation is also known as *document building, document assembly* or *merging*.

boot up To prepare the computer for use as a word processor by inserting the necessary disk(s) and pressing the appropriate key(s) to load the program into the system.

borders Ornamental borders may be created by using combinations of alphabet characters, numbers or symbols to create an artistic design around sections of text, eg, material marked on page 12.

&£&£&£&£&£&£&£ #*#*#*#*#*#*

)()()()()()()(%@%@%@%@%@%@%

borders

This type of decoration is suitable for menus, advertisements and newsletters. (See **decoration** and **tailpiece.**)

******   ******
**   **
*   *

THE GOURMET'S RETREAT

BUSINESS LUNCH

M E N U

Oxtail Soup
Grapefruit and Melon Cocktail
Fruit Juice

****

Vegetable Lasagne
Steak and Kidney Pie
Roast Lamb

****

Vegetables in Season
French Fries or Boiled Potatoes

****

Fresh Fruit Salad and Cream
Blackcurrant Cheesecake
Cheese and Biscuits

****

Coffee or Tea

****
*****
***
*

*   *
**   **
******   ******

borders

boxed table Horizontal and vertical lines may be drawn around information displayed as a table of columns and rows to separate it from the body of the text. Type the horizontal lines by using the underscore key and rule the vertical lines in ink on the completed document. Additional vertical lines may be ruled in the column spaces to separate the columns.

S P R I N G D E S I G N S

Garment	Style	Colour	Sizes	
			Adult	Child
Pyjamas	Tracey	Pink	S,M,L	10-12
Nightshirt	Louella	Blue	S,M	8-12
Nightdress	Carolina	Cream	S,M,L	12-14

boxed table

brace A left facing brace {, or a right facing brace }, is used to link two or more lines of text. A left facing brace is formed on the typewriter or word processor by typing the left bracket character at the same scale point at the start of each line of text. A right facing brace is formed by typing the right bracket at the same scale point at the end of each line of text.

```
                    (Information is typed close
Left facing brace   (up to the brackets used to
                    (form the brace.

Leave at least one clear space after)
the brackets before starting to type) Right facing brace
the details alongside the brace.    )
```

brace

brackets A bracket, or pair of brackets, may be used to separate a paragraph number or letter from the text of the paragraph, eg, 1) or a), (1) or (a). Brackets are also used around sections of text, a left bracket being placed before the text and a right bracket at the end of the text. Do not leave a space between the bracket and the text to which it is related.

Brackets are sometimes referred to as parentheses.

brightness control The brightness of the VDU screen can be adjusted to suit the operator and the lighting conditions in the room. Some screens also have a contrast control to adjust the contrast between the text and the background screen colour.

bring forward file (See **reminder file**.)

buffer memory A specific area in the memory storage of a word processor where text is saved as a temporary measure such as in the cut and paste or copy functions.

business documents A wide range of documents is involved in business transactions, including the price list, enquiry, quotation, purchase order, advice note, delivery note, invoice, statement, credit note and debit note.

C

camera ready copy (crc) Typescript material produced by a daisywheel printer using a carbon ribbon, or by a laser printer, that is ready for photographing as part of the printing process and does not need to be typeset.

capitals To type a single capital letter, hold down the shift key while typing the character key for which a capital letter is required. To type continuous text in capitals, activate the shift lock key and type the text required. When you have typed all the words that are to be printed in capitals, press the shift lock key once more to de-activate it.

Some keys, such as the number keys on the top row, are labelled with more than one character. When the shift key or the shift lock key are depressed, the uppermost character will be printed.

Most computer keyboards also contain a *caps lock* key. When this is activated the alphabet characters are printed as capitals, but all other keys are unaffected, and the lower character/symbol will be printed even when the caps lock is activated.

Some computer keyboards include a special key to allow text to be changed automatically from capitals to lower-case letters and vice versa.

Leave one space between words typed in capitals. If words are typed in spaced capitals, leave one space between the characters of a word and three spaces between words.

caps lock (capitals lock) A key found on some word processing keyboards that, when depressed, converts all the alphabet characters on the keyboard to upper-case (capitals). The number keys are not affected by the use of the caps lock key. If you wish to type the symbols that appear above the numbers on the top row of keys you must press the shift key. The caps lock key is pressed to activate the capitals and pressed again to return to lower-case characters. (See **shift key**.)

carbon copy A duplicate of a document which is produced simultaneously with the master document, generally to provide a copy of the original document for the files for future reference.

To make one carbon copy you need two pieces of paper and a sheet of carbon-coated paper. Place the sheet of carbon paper between the two sheets of paper with the carbon-coated surface facing away from the top sheet of paper. Place the pack of three sheets into the machine with the carbon-coated side of the carbon paper facing towards the typewriter roller. Text typed on to the top sheet of paper, is automatically duplicated (copied) on to the sheet below the carbon paper.

About five or six copies may be made simultaneously in this way, but the quality of the copy deteriorates with each additional sheet of carbon paper and copy paper.

Carbon copying is used mainly on typewriters. If carbon copies are required on word processor or computer printers, specially prepared continuous carbon sets, or NCR (no carbon required) paper is generally used.

carbon paper A special paper, one side of which is coated with a carbon duplicating medium, which is used to produce a copy of a special document when it is typed.

card holder Plastic card holder attachments are fitted close to the alignment scale on many typewriters to ensure that cards such as postcards or indexing cards are held firmly in place while you type.

care of equipment Typewriters and word processors should be cleaned regularly to ensure continuous good performance. Ensure that electrical equipment is switched off before carrying out any cleaning operations. Use a lint-free duster and appropriate cleaning agent to clean the casing of all equipment. The VDU screen may be cleaned with a special anti-static solution. Some people recommend the use of special disks for cleaning the disk drives of a word processor. Cleaning of other parts of the equipment is generally included in the routine maintenance and service care carried out by a service engineer. You should not attempt to clean the inside of any equipment.

Carefully clean the typeface of a manual typewriter with a stiff brush to remove the build-up of ink deposits. The daisywheel printheads used on electronic typewriters and word processors may be placed in a special cleaning solution to remove ink deposits. Do not use a brush on these printheads because they are fragile and easily broken.

carriage return The return of the typing point to the left-hand margin. This operation is accompanied by an advance of the paper by one line space on manual, electric and electronic typewriters. The carriage return lever is used for this purpose on a manual typewriter. The return key is used on electric and electronic typewriters.

There are two types of return on a word processor. The *hard return* entered by using the return or enter key, is the equivalent of a carriage return on a typewriter. It will remain in position no matter how much editing is done, until the operator gives a command to remove the return.

A *soft return* is the 'wraparound' return automatically inserted at the end of a line of type in continuous text. The return is 'soft' in the sense that the word processor can automatically make adjustments to the line endings if the text is edited.

case sensitive A word processing term referring to the use of upper-case or lower-case characters (ie capitals or small letters). When carrying out certain functions some word processing systems will recognise a text item only if it is typed in the same 'case'. For example, to recall a document to the screen you may key in the name SALES REPORT. If the system is case sensitive it will not find the name if it was originally keyed in as Sales Report. The same problem may arise on some systems with the search and replace function. A system that is not case sensitive will find *any case* and may also find *any attribute*, ie underlined or emboldened.

catchword If a document consists of two or more pages, some people like to use a catchword in the bottom right margin of each page. An oblique stroke is typed, followed by the first word that will appear on the next page. The use of catchwords in this way has little value in assisting the reader, and you should use them only if you are requested by the author to do so.

central processing unit (CPU) The part of a computer or word processor that controls the processes it performs. It also contains a memory where the program being used is stored and where work being carried out is stored until it is saved to the working disk.

centring The placement of text midway between two points. Text may be horizontally and/or vertically centred on the page.

Horizontal centring Text positioned midway between the left and right edges of the paper, or between equal margins, is said to be horizontally centred. If unequal margins are used (eg, a wide left margin and a narrow right margin), the text is centred 'over the typing line' ie between the two margin settings. If you use a typewriter, calculate the centre point between the margins set, move the typing point to this position and backspace once for every two characters or spaces of the text to be centred. This becomes the starting point for the line of text. An automatic centring function is provided on electronic typewriters and word processors. Not all word processing systems display the text as centred on the screen, but those that do are more helpful to the typist.

Vertical centring When the text is positioned midway between the top and bottom edges of the paper, it is said to be *vertically centred.* Count the number of lines of text and the spaces between them. Subtract this number from the number of line spaces available on the page. Divide the remaining number by 2, and leave this number of line spaces above the text. If, for example, the text and clear line spaces between occupy 44 line spaces, subtract 44 from 70 (the number of line spaces available on an A4 page at 6 line spaces to the inch). Divide the remaining 26 spaces by 2, giving the result of 13 line spaces. Turn down 14 times before starting to type. This will give a top margin of 13 clear line spaces. If you use a word processor, remember that the word processor will automatically provide for a top margin space of 6 or 7 line spaces in the default setting.

CHAMBERLINE COPYHOLDERS

A full range of copyholders to suit every purpose

MAN-LINE COPYHOLDER

Our basic model - a free-standing, desktop copyholder with a manually-adjustable linefinder and a slim but stable base.

Lines of text PLUS Clear line spaces 28 16 = 44

NU-LINE COPYHOLDER

This is similar to the Man-line copyholder but line-by-line downward movement of the linefinder is controlled by a pneumatically-operated foot pedal for greater convenience and ease of use.

Line spaces available on A4 LESS Lines to be used 70 44 = 26

CLAMP-LINE

The basic clamp model fastens onto the edge of the desk and its flexible arm allows the copyholder plate to be adjusted to the position most suitable for the operator.

WIDE-LINE COPYHOLDER

Designed to take larger sheets of paper, the plate of this model extends on a swing-arm mechanism to give maximum mobility and adjustment to suit the operator. The copyholder clamps firmly to the edge of the desk.

Line spaces available for top and bottom margins 26 ÷ 2 = 13

AIR-LINE COPYHOLDER

The air-operated foot pedal of this model moves the linefinder down to the next line, and spacing between lines can be adjusted as required. The copyholder clamps to the edge of the desk and its counterbalanced arm facilitates easy movement.

calculations for vertical headings

change bars A word processing function whereby changes made to a document during the editing process are highlighted by a bar or vertical line printed at the left and right margin positions. Change bars can be helpful to an author for comparing editing changes with the original draft. (See **revision tracking**.)

character set The characters, figures and symbols available on a particular keyboard. The character set provided on an electronic keyboard generally contains a number of symbols that are not available on the keyboard of a manual typewriter, eg, < > # \ { }.

a b c d e f g h i j k l m n o p q r s t u v w x y z A B C D E F G H I J K L
M N O P Q R S T U V W X Y Z 1 2 3 4 5 6 7 8 9 0 – ¾ ⅜ = ⅞ ⅔ , . ; : ½ *
" / @ £ _ & ' ( ) ? ¼ ⅛ + ⅝ ⅓ % # ¥ $ ° ¢ ! $^{2\,3}$ |

a b c d e f g h i j k l m n o p q r s t u v w x y z A B C D E F G H I J K L
M N O P Q R S T U V W X Y Z 1 2 3 4 5 6 7 8 9 0 – = ! @ £ $ % ° &
* ( ) – + [ ] { } ; ‹ : › " / ' ? \ ~ | § # ° ¡ ™ ¢ ∞ ° ¶ • ª º – ≠ " œ π Ø □ .
¥ † ® ' Σ å © △ — ... æ ' ÷ ≷ ≶ μ ƒ √ ç ≈ Ω «

character set

chart (See **graph**.)

check index When you save a word processing document to your working disk the name you have allocated to it will appear in the index or directory. Before logging off from your word processing program always check the index to be sure that you have saved your documents to the working disk and not to the system disk.

check space on disk There is a limit to the amount of data that can be stored on any electronic storage media, such as floppy disks. It is good practice to check the amount of space available on a disk before starting work. Most word processing systems provide some method of ascertaining the amount of space left on a disk. This may be given in terms of the number of A4 pages or the number of kilobytes available on the disk. You should never attempt to fill the disk completely, and should generally leave about 25 pages free in case it is later necessary to edit or add to the existing text stored on the disk. Some systems display an operator prompt on the screen when disk space is running low.

chip (See **microchip**.)

chronological order A sorting category that involves placing items in date or time order. Items may be sorted chronologically in ascending order, eg, January to December, 1992 to 1999 or 9.30 am to 5.30 pm, or in descending order, eg, December to January, 1999 to 1992 or 5.30 pm to 9.30 am.

circular letter A letter that is copied or duplicated and sent to a large number of people is known as a circular letter. Many circular letters are impersonal, ie they are addressed to *Dear Sir, Dear Madam* or *Dear Customer.* The date is sometimes omitted from a standard circular letter, or it may be included as 'month and year only' (eg, June 1995). Alternatively the words 'Date as Postmark' may be inserted. Many companies use the mailmerge function of a word processor to personalise circular letters by adding the name and address of the recipient to each letter.

ROCKLINE CATERING SERVICES

14 RESTON DRIVE TIMEWELL COVENTRY CV14 8RJ

Telephone: 447260

Partners: Sara and Giles Rock

Our ref GMR/EBJ

June 199-

Dear Sir

BUSINESS CATERING

We are pleased to announce our new Business Catering enterprise, specially designed to save time and money for your company, while at the same time providing an efficient and personal service.

We can supply anything from a few simple, but delicious, sandwiches or boxed lunches to a full-scale buffet or conference dinner. Our foods are all produced by expert, trained staff in our own kitchens with the best ingredients. Appearance of the finished produce is considered as important as quality, and we pride ourselves on our attractive table layouts.

The attached schedule of menus and prices will give you some idea of our wide range and competitive pricing policy.

In addition we are happy to supply anything, however unusual, to meet any special needs you may have. Just contact Sara or Giles at the above number for advice or a quotation.

Yours faithfully
ROCKLINE CATERING SERVICES

Giles Rock

Enc

circular letter

circulation list A list of names of people who are to receive a single document such as a report or a magazine. The copy of the document will be passed from one person to another to avoid the need for multiple copies to be made. The circulation list may be printed on a circulation slip and attached to the document, and as soon as an individual has finished reading it he or she will initial and date the slip and pass it on, as shown in the example below.

CIRCULATION LIST Please read this document and pass it on as quickly as possible.		
	INITIALS	DATE
G Arthur	[illegible]	15 Sept
L Cranston	L. C.	17 Sept.
B R Hebden	BRH	18 SEP.
R James		
E A Lewis		
S T Young		

circulation list

The term circulation list is sometimes used to indicate a list of all the people who receive an individual copy of a document, although this is, strictly speaking, a distribution list. (See **distribution list.**)

clear line space A line space that has no text typed on it. To leave one clear line space between items press the return key twice when single line spacing is set. This gives one clear line and a line that will be typed on. To leave two clear lines spaces press the return key three times. To leave three clear line spaces press the return key four times, and so on.

coded space (See **protected space.**)

column movement Some word processors allow the operator to move columns from one location on the screen display to another.

The block of text that forms the column to be moved is marked out by inserting coded symbols, or by highlighting the text in reverse video. It is then cut from its original position on the screen and pasted into its new position.

Alternatively, on some systems it may be 'walked' across the screen display.

columns A column is vertical presentation of figures and/or text. Two or more columns are separated by a column space. In a table of several columns, leave equal spacing between the columns.

combination characters Characters that are formed when using a typewriter by typing two characters, one on top of another, to give a letter or symbol that is not available on the keyboard, eg:

S	plus	/	gives	$	(dollar)
c	plus	/	gives	¢	(cent)
c	plus	,	gives	ç	(cedilla)
Y	plus	=	gives	¥	(yen)

communications The term communications is used in connection with information processing to refer to the passing of information from one computer-based system to another by electronic means. This covers the use of systems such as telex, electronic mail and messaging systems, video conferencing, videotex and viewdata.

Word processors are used extensively for electronic mailing. Messages may be passed from one word processor to another. Alternatively, the message may be mailed to a computer mailbox, where it is stored by the computer until the recipient accesses the mailbox to see if any messages have been left.

The operator needs to input address details, known as *the envelope,* followed by the message, known as the *contents.* Once the command to despatch the message has been given, the 'mail' is sent automatically to a single receiving terminal or simultaneously to a number of terminals, which may be in the same building or in a remote location in another country. With many systems the sender is able to check to see if the message has been received by the addressee.

complimentary close The formal ending of a letter, eg, *Yours sincerely* or *Yours faithfully,* which is followed by the writer's signature and/or designation (job title).

compliment slip A small piece of paper, generally A6 size, on which the name and address of a company are printed together with the words *With the compliments of.* There is generally space for a brief message and a signature. Compliment slips are used in place of a letter when only an informal note is required containing a remark such as *Here is the report I promised to send.*

consumable supplies Those supplies, such as paper, envelopes, printer ribbons, that are used and then replaced. Floppy disks are generally included under the term *consumable supplies.*

continuation sheet The second and subsequent pages of a document are known as continuation sheets. Continuation sheets of documents such as reports should always contain the page number. In addition they may contain running header and/or running footer details such as the date, a reference number or the title of the report.

The continuation sheet of a letter should not be typed on printed letterheaded paper. Use plain paper of a matching size and quality, or specially printed continuation sheet stationery if this is provided by the company you work for. Type the page number, the addressee's name and the date at the left margin at the top of each continuation sheet. If you use a word processor these details may be stored in the header area so that they are automatically printed on each continuation sheet.

copy If you use a typewriter, you will use either carbon paper or a photocopier to produce a copy of your documents. If you use a word processor, the term *copy* is applied to functions for making a duplicate of a block of text, a document or a disk.

Copy a block When you copy a block or section of a document on the word processor, you make use of both the copy and paste functions, even if the actual term *paste* is not used. To copy a block of text or data, identify the section to be copied by inserting coded symbols at the start and end of the block, or by highlighting it in reverse video. Key in the command to instruct the system to copy the block. Move the cursor to the position at which the block of text is to be inserted and key in the command to paste in the copy.

Copy a document In word processing terms this refers to the duplication of a document or file that has been stored on the disk. The copying procedure may be carried out from the index or the main menu. The name of the document to be duplicated is keyed in, together with a new name for the copy, and the command to copy is given.

Copy a disk Copies should be made of both program disks and working disks in case a disk is accidentally damaged or lost. These are referred to as back-up copies, security copies or archive disks. The procedure for copying a disk varies from one system to another. It is a good idea to stick a *write-protect* label in the correct position over the write-enable notch on the disk to be copied so that you cannot accidentally overwrite it by copying the blank disk on to it. Label the copied disks clearly as copies for identification purposes.

copy and paste A word processing function for copying a section of text and pasting (inserting) it into another part of the same document, or of another document. The copied section of text remains in its original position, unlike the cut and paste function where the section of text is actually cut and moved to a new position. The copy and paste function is useful where text has to be repeated several times, for repeating horizontal lines in a table without having to key them in each time or for rows of dotted lines on a form. (See **cut and paste.**)

copyholder A device for holding material which is to be copied by the typist. A good copyholder is designed to hold the material to be copied at eye-level. Electrically operated copyholders incorporate a line marker to indicate the line being typed, and the marker is automatically moved down the page when a foot pedal is depressed. Some copyholders incorporate a light at the top of the holder to illuminate the task being worked on.

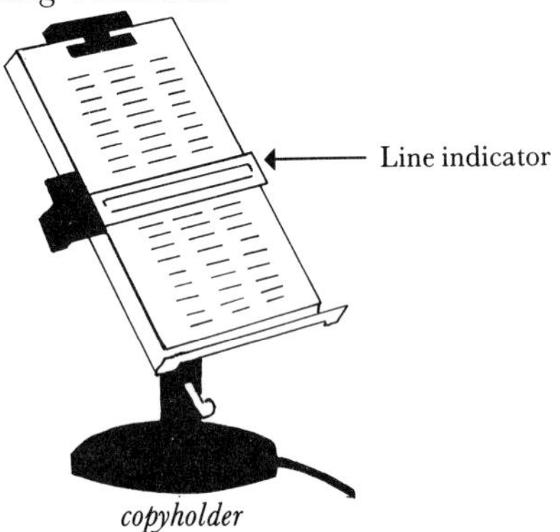

copyholder

copyright The right to copy, or permit copying of, a document, play, book, computer program and many other works rests with the author or publisher. The law relating to copyright is fairly complex, but typists and word processor operators should be aware that program disks, user manuals and other documents should not be copied without the permission of the computer software company, the publisher or the author. In the case of computer program disks, permission is usually granted to the purchaser to make a copy of the disk for security purposes, in case the original disk is damaged or lost.

correction ribbon (See **corrections.**)

corrections Corrections made to a typewritten document should be as unobtrusive as possible. An error is most easily corrected as soon as it is made (ie, before the paper is removed from the typewriter), and many people prefer to read through their work before removing the paper from the machine. A correction made after the paper has been removed from the typewriter involves careful re-alignment of the line of type when the paper is replaced in the typewriter. A number of different correction methods are available, including special fluid, paper and tape. Rubber erasers are rarely used nowadays because they damage the surface of the paper and produce a less satisfactory correction than that produced by modern correcting media.

Correction fluid Correction fluid is available in white, or in a variety of colours for use on coloured papers. Paint the fluid sparingly over the error and allow it to dry before typing the correct character(s).

Correction paper Slips of specially coated paper may be used. Place the correction paper over the error and type the incorrect character(s) so that the coating covers the outline of the typed character. Remove the correction paper, use the backspace key to move the typing point to the appropriate position and type the correct character(s).

Correction ribbon Many electric and electronic typewriters may be fitted with a special correction ribbon, in addition to the inked ribbon. There are two types of ribbon: *lift-off*, which is used with a carbon ribbon, and *cover-up*, which is used with a fabric ribbon. The lift-off ribbon removes the printed character from the paper when a special key is pressed, and the correct character can then be typed in its place. The cover-up ribbon deposits a white coating over the incorrect characters and the correct characters are typed on top of this deposit.

Corrections are easily made on a word processor because any errors identified when proofreading on the screen may be changed using the editing functions before the document is printed. If you find any errors when the document is printed, correct them on the screen document and then print it again.

correction signs A range of standard correction signs, or editing marks, are used to indicate changes that should be made to a handwritten, typewritten or printed document when it is re-typed. The most frequently used signs are shown below.

CORRECTION SIGNS

MEANING	SIGN	EXAMPLE
Insert text	⋏	Insert a ⋏ word here and a char⋏ a cter here.
Insert a space	/	An oblique stroke indicates that a space is/needed between words, as shown/here. Alternatively, a hash sign may⋏be # written in the margin to show that a space is⋏required. #
	#	
Close up a space	⁐	Too much ⁐ space ⁐ - ⁐ close it up.
Use capitals	CAPS	Type the word (urgent) at the top. CAPS
Use upper case (capital letters)	UC	The health and safety committee. UC

Use lower case (small letters)	lc	Send a Form to claim your Expenses. lc
Let the original text stand	✓	The work is completed. ✓ These new figures are incorrect. ✓
Delete the text that has been crossed out		The Editors of the company's house magazine has asked as many members of staff as possible to contribute.
Transpose words or characters (ie, change their positions)		Ask your manager to sign form number BD/4723 and send it to the Training Officer for action and approval.
Transpose sections of text (ie, change their positions)		1 2 Training in First Aid will be given during working hours. 2 1 All members of staff will be encouraged to attend First Aid training courses.
Begin a new paragraph	[//	There are two signs to indicate the start of a new paragraph. [One is a sign like a square bracket, as shown at the start of this sentence. //The other sign consists of two oblique lines, as shown at the start of this sentence.
Join two paragraphs together (run on).		It may be necessary to join two paragraphs. This is done by linking them with a continuous line, as shown here.

courtesy titles The abbreviation or word used before a person's name to indicate his or her status or position, such as Mr, Mrs, Ms, Dr, Sir or Professor. A courtesy title should be used in the addressee details of a letter and in the salutation, eg. *Dear Mr Adams* or *Dear Sir Lawrence*.

currency symbols Only a few of the symbols used to represent currency are available on the keyboard and these generally include: £ (pound sterling), $ (dollar USA), and ¥ (Yen Japan). Symbols may be combined with alphabet characters to form, for example, A$ (Australian dollar) and IR£ (punt Republic of Ireland). If a currency symbol is not available on the keyboard, leave a space at the appropriate point and write the symbol in ink on the completed document, or type the name of the currency in full. (See **combination characters**.)

SOME OVERSEAS CURRENCIES

Angola	Kwanza	Kz	Ecuador	Sucre	Su
Argentina	Austral	Arg$	Egypt	Pound	E£
Australia	Dollar	A$	France	Franc	Fr
Austria	Schilling	Sch	Fiji	Dollar	F$
Barbados	Dollar	Bds$	Hong Kong	Dollar	HK$
Belgium	Franc	BFr	Jamaica	Dollar	J$
Bolivia	Peso	B$	Japan	Yen	¥
Burma	Kyat	K	New Zealand	Dollar	NZ$
Canada	Dollar	C$	Poland	Zloty	Zl
Cyprus	Pound	C£	Sudan	Pound	S£
Denmark	Krone	DKr	Zimbabwe	Dollar	Z$

list of currencies

curriculum vitae A document listing, in date order, the details of a person's educational and employment record and any other details considered appropriate. A curriculum vitae (or CV) is most frequently used in connection with job applications.

cursor The marker displayed on a word processor or computer screen to indicate the point at which the next character will appear when a key is pressed. The cursor may consist of a small block or a line, and it may or may not flash to ensure that it is easily identified.

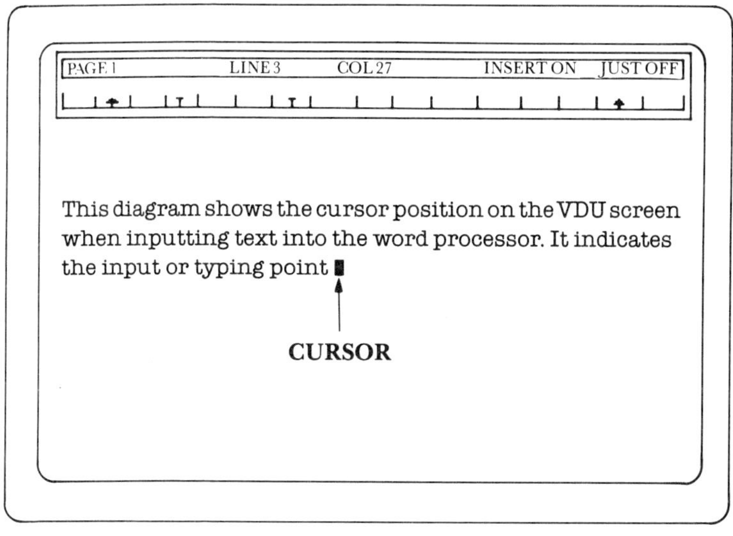

the cursor

cursor movement The cursor may be moved anywhere on the screen by use of special cursor movement keys, which are generally positioned to the right of the QWERTY keyboard.

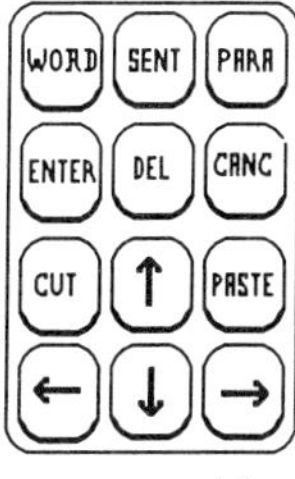

cursor control keys

There are usually four keys, each labelled with an arrow indicating the direction of movement of the cursor when the key is pressed, ie right, left, up, down. It may also be possible to move the cursor forward or backward by a word at a time, or a line, sentence or paragraph at a time. The cursor moves once in the direction of the arrow each time the key is pressed. Continuous pressure on the key produces continuous movement of the cursor. When a word processing program is used on some types of microcomputer, it is necessary to use a combination of code and alphabet character keys if dedicated cursor keys are not available.

cut A word processing function that allows a word, sentence or block of text to be cut out of the document. Unless you give the system further instructions, the text that has been cut is then deleted from the document. If the text that has been cut is to be used again, it is stored in either a temporary or permanent memory area until a command is given to 'paste' it into the same document or another document.

cut and paste A pair of word processing functions that allow text to be cut from a document and pasted in again at a new position, either in the same document or in another document. Once the text has been cut, the paste command may generally be used several times to paste the text in again repeatedly at the point identified by the position of the cursor.

cut column A word processor function that allows a vertical column of text or figures to be cut from a table, leaving the other columns in place. The column that has been cut may be moved and pasted in again at a different position in the table, or in another document, or it may be deleted.

D

daisywheel A flat circular printhead, made of plastic or metal, for use with an electronic typewriter or word processor printer. The printwheel, which is shaped something like a daisy flower, has characters embossed on the end of each 'petal'. A hammer strikes a petal against the ribbon to print a character on the paper. Daisywheels are available with many different styles of type (fonts) and type sizes (pitch) and they may be changed quickly and easily if a different pitch or font is required. It is useful to have several different types of daisywheel in stock, and to have a spare daisywheel containing the typestyle most frequently used, in case one is damaged.

Plastic daisywheels are fairly delicate and should be handled with care. Do not handle them by the 'spokes' of the wheel—always hold the central portion. Keep daisywheels that are not being used in a storage container. It is useful to label the containers so that you can find the one you want quickly when necessary. Metal daisywheels last longer than plastic ones, and are stronger, but they should still be handled with care.

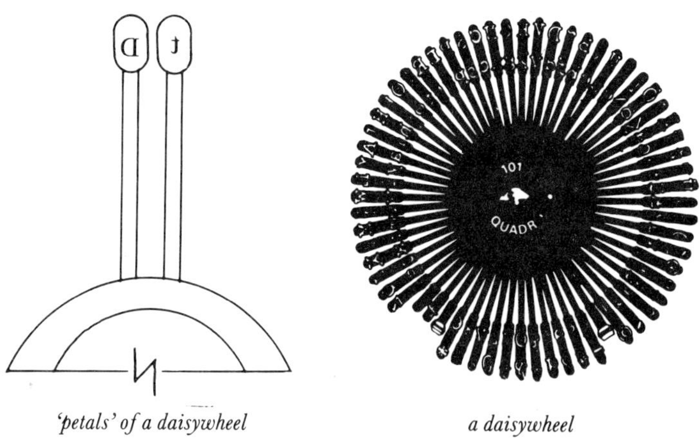

'petals' of a daisywheel *a daisywheel*

dash The dash is represented in typewriting by using the hyphen key with a clear character space each side of it.

data In general terms the word 'data' is used to refer to information in the form of numbers, characters and symbols that can be stored, processed or produced by a computer. Images, in the form of drawings, maps or photographs, may also be stored and manipulated on computers, and these form another category of data.

databank An organised collection of information stored electronically, ready for access by computer users. The term databank is often used as an alternative name for a *database,* but it generally implies that much more information is stored than in a database. Vast quantities of information can be stored in a database and retrieved, or accessed, at very high speeds.

Prestel, Ceefax and Eurolex services allow users to access information in their very large databanks and view them on a VDU or television screen. Databanks such as Prestel are public systems; this means that anyone with the appropriate equipment is able to access the information, some of which is supplied free of charge and some of which must be paid for. The details in many other databases are available only to specific groups of people. The information in the Eurolex databank, for example, is available to people such as lawyers who pay a subscription to use the service (See **viewdata.**)

database A collection of information stored on a computer by means of a database program, and organised in such a way that it is easy for a user to search for and display selected items of the stored data on a VDU screen. The term database may sometimes be used as an alternative for databank, and a database program is often called a database management system (or DBMS). Data stored in a database usually relates to a particular topic area in an organisation, such as personnel records, customer details or stock lists.

Access to the database information by subscribers or other authorised persons may be restricted to one or more of the following categories for security reasons.

Read only or *read and print* Information may be called to the screen and read and/or printed.

Read and interact Information may be called to the screen and read. In response to questions or prompts the user may then input information, such as an order for goods or reservation of an aircraft seat.

Amend The user can read, print and amend the data in the database. Only authorised people can access the database at this level, to update the information.

data processing The manipulation of data, generally by a computer, in the form of numbers or text. Mathematical calculations may be carried out on data in the form of numbers, or information may be sorted, selected or otherwise manipulated.

Data Protection Act 1984 Any person holding information electronically in a computer about any other person or business must register with the Data Protection Registrar. There are certain exceptions to this regulation, but individuals or organisations holding records of this type on computer should check with the Data Protection Registrar if they wish to be sure that they are exempted.

The *Data Protection Act* lays down certain rules covering the type of information being held, how it is to be used, whether it will be transferred to a second person within or outside the United Kingdom, how access to the information is to be controlled and so on.

Individuals who are concerned about the type and accuracy of information being held about them in a company's computer file can ask to see a copy of the information,and this must be provided by the organisation on payment of a fee. There are exceptions to this general rule, particularly in connection with state-controlled organisations. Details about the provisions and operation of this Act may be obtained from the Data Protection Registrar, Wilmslow, SK9 5AX.

date All correspondence, such as formal business letters, informal personal letters or memoranda, should include the current date, ie the date on which the correspondence was typed. This information is essential when people are answering a letter, or when they wish to refer back to a particular letter in the files. Correspondence is usually filed in date order, which is also known as chronological order. You should always include the date on correspondence, even if you are not given a direct instruction to do so.

Type the date in full in the order of day, month and year, eg, 17 September 1994. Modern practice is to omit *st, nd, rd, th* after the number of the day, ie type 1, 2, 3, 4 *not* 1st, 2nd, 3rd, 4th.

When the block style of layout is used the date is usually typed at the left-hand margin between the reference and the name and address of the recipient. As an acceptable alternative the date may be typed on the right-hand side of the page, opposite to the recipient's address.

In circular letters the month and year only may be typed, eg, June 1994, so that the letters remain current throughout the whole of a month. In other cases the words *Date as Postmark* may be used on circular letters.

In overseas countries, particularly those following the practice of the United States of America, the date is typed in the order of month, day and year, eg, April 9 1994. If the date is shown all in figures there is a possibility of confusion, eg, 4/9/94 is April 9 1994 in America but 4 September 1994 in the United Kingdom.

Some word processors have an automatic date-insertion facility that will enter the correct date on a document when the appropriate command is given.

dead keys (See **accents.**)

decoration (Also known as **ornamentation**) Certain types of document, such as menus, programmes and notices, may be enhanced by the addition of decoration. A variety of symbol or character keys can be used to produce borders or patterns, eg, *************)()()()()()(or %$%$%$%$%$%. It is also possible to produce pictures by using a variety of keys, and some of these pictures involve overtyping one character over another.

Decoration can add to the appeal of a document, but it should be used sparingly, bearing in mind that the message incorporated in the text is of the main importance.

dedicated function keys Instructions or commands are keyed in to a word processor by the operator to tell it to carry out certain functions such as centring, underlining or copying text. This may be done by pressing two or more keys, known as a key sequence. On some word processing systems it may be necessary to press three or four character keys to input a command. In these cases the character keys perform two functions. They act as character keys for inputting text and, in conjunction with a coding key, they also act as command keys for carrying out operations or functions. Other systems are provided with special keys programmed (or dedicated) to carry out a particular function and labelled appropriately. These programmed function keys, known as dedicated keys, may include functions such as centre, copy, cut, embolden, help, indent, paste, replace, search, underline and undo.

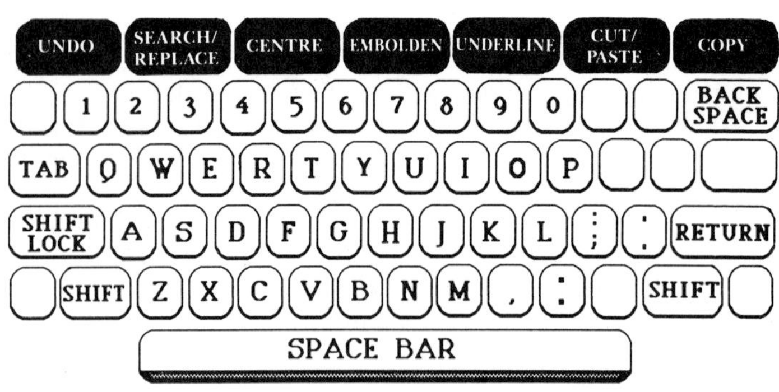

dedicated function keys

dedicated word processor A computer programmed specifically for word processing, as compared with a general-purpose computer that may (by using the appropriate programs) carry out a range of office functions such as database, spreadsheet, word processing, communications and presentation graphics. The keyboard of a dedicated word processor will generally contain *dedicated function keys*. Many people claim that a dedicated word processor is easier to use than a computer operating with a word processing program. It may also include a greater number of word processing functions than a computer using a word processing program.

default A term used in word processing indicating that certain settings have been written into the program, and that these settings will be used if the operator does not override them. In other words, the pre-programmed settings will be used *in default* of the operator choosing alternative settings. This ensures that text can be processed and printed in a usable form even if the operator fails to select new settings.

Default settings on a word processor include items such as margins, tab stops, line spacing, print size, page length, justified or ragged right margin and insert or overtype mode. The default settings may be checked by referring to the system's user manual, which will also explain the procedures for changing these settings to suit the requirements of the operator.

delete a disk It may sometimes be necessary to delete *all* the documents from a disk. Deleting all the files individually can take a long time, and an alternative method should be used. You can delete the disk by reformatting it or by copying a blank disk on to the disk that is to be deleted. When the disk has been cleared, replace the existing identification label with a new label indicating that the disk is empty and ready for use.

delete a document or file A document, or file, is generally deleted from the index, or directory, through the main menu. Documents that are no longer required are deleted as part of the general housekeeping procedure, so that only essential files are kept on the disk, and to clear storage space for new documents.

The option to delete or cut a document (file) from the directory is selected from the menu. A system prompt will ask the operator to give the name of the file to be deleted. When this has been keyed in, the command to delete the file is given. Care must be taken to ensure that the correct file is selected for deletion, because a deleted file cannot be recalled on most systems. Many word processing systems display an operator prompt on the screen when the command to delete has been given, asking, for example; 'Are you sure you wish to delete this file?' This gives the operator the opportunity to cancel the command if an error has been made. If there is no error, the delete command is repeated and the file is cleared from the disk.

delete text A word processing function for removing a character, word or section of text, by using either the backspace delete key, the dedicated delete function key(s) or the necessary key sequence for deletion of text.

Text may be deleted immediately after it has been typed, simply by pressing the backspace delete key, which moves the cursor from right to left across the screen, deleting a character at a time. This method of deletion is usually used to correct typing errors immediately they have been made. If you notice a typing error in text that has already been keyed in, move the cursor to the space immediately to the right of the incorrect character(s), press the backspace delete key as many times as necessary and then key in the correct character(s). Alternatively, you can move the cursor so that it rests on the incorrect character(s) and change from insert mode to overtype mode. Any character(s) you key in will automatically delete and replace the characters already on the screen. The overtype mode should be used with care when making corrections in this way, to ensure that you do not accidentally type over text that should remain on the screen. Always remember to change back from overtype to insert mode as soon as you have made the necessary amendments.

The backspace delete key is most useful for deleting a small number of characters. On many systems there are special keys, or key sequences, for deleting a word, line, sentence, paragraph or larger block of text. They may go under the name 'delete' or they may be part of the 'cut' function. Care must be taken when deleting or cutting large sections of text to ensure that the correct part of the text is being deleted, otherwise it could be permanently lost. Some systems have an 'undo' command which will allow you to undo the last command, and this would permit you to recall any text deleted in error.

descenders The part of the lower-case characters g, j, p, q, and y that extend below the main part of the character and 'descend' below the line of type.

desktop publishing Desktop publishing systems, usually referred to by the abbreviated name of DTP systems, are a means of page layout and production to typesetting standards from equipment that is small enough to be put on a desk. Complete pages of information, including text, pictures and graphics are prepared on a computer screen from facilities built into a sophisticated computer program. The page layout that has been prepared is then printed, generally by means of a laser printer, as *camera ready copy* (ie ready for printing in bulk).

A DTP system consists of a microcomputer, page layout software and a laser printer, which can reproduce the pages exactly as they are shown on the screen. The microcomputer can be a standalone system, or part of a networked configuration. The computer program is capable of combining word processing facilities with graphics and line art, and of mixing typestyles and type sizes. The text and pictures can be moved about the screen to place the text in columns and to position the pictures next to the appropriate text.

DTP systems allow personal computer users to produce professional-looking documents for a fraction of the cost of conventional typesetting and printing.

destination disk This term is used in word processing procedures such as copying disks. When instructions are given in the user manual, it is necessary to identify the various disks that will be used so that the operator knows exactly which disk to insert into the disk drive at any time. In a procedure such as copying a disk, the disk containing the material to be copied is called the source disk, and the disk to which the material is to be copied is called the destination disk.

destination document If you are copying text from one document to another, the terms source document and destination document are used to clarify the instructions for carrying out the procedure. The destination document is the document into which you wish to insert text from another document (See **boilerplating**.)

diary systems Computer diary programs allow an individual to keep a record of appointments, meetings, reminders, etc, on disk. The diary can be viewed and updated on screen when required, and if necessary a printout can be obtained of whole days or weeks of the diary, or of selected appointments. More sophisticated diary programs for groups of people are often referred to as time management systems. These are operated by means of computers linked together through a local area network (LAN). Time management systems allow a user to access and view the diary of another person, or several other people. This is useful, for example, if you want to check if a number of people are free for a meeting at a particular time, or to find out where a certain person will be on a given date.

Diary systems will only work effectively if all users keep their electronic diaries up to date.

dictionary A word processing dictionary, or spelling checker, is a program, or part of a program, that contains a list of correctly spelt words. When the operator instructs the word processor to check a document for any possible spelling errors, the program checks each word against the list of words stored in the computer memory. Any word that is not contained in this list will be identified in some way by the system, often by highlighting in reverse video.

The highlighted word may be a spelling error, but it may also be a word that is not contained in the dictionary. Because of limited storage space, the dictionary may contain only a few thousand words (as compared with about 200 000 words in many printed dictionaries). The system therefore identifies the word as a possible error. The word may in fact be spelt correctly, and the operator will have to check the spelling by referring to a printed dictionary. Alternatively, the word may be a name, eg, the name of a company or product.

The operator is then given the option of altering the spelling or of accepting it. If, for example, the highlighted word is a name, the operator presses a key to accept the spelling as shown and the system moves on, checking each word until another possible error is identified. Some word processing dictionaries will even display an operator prompt suggesting the correct spelling of the word.

Additional dictionaries are available for specialist areas such as medical or technical work. The operator can usually add extra words to such dictionaries to increase their usefulness.

The majority of word processing dictionaries are not able to identify grammatical errors such as the use of *where* for *were,* or *their* for *there,* because each word is spelt correctly but is simply used in the wrong context. Spelling check dictionaries are therefore useful for helping the operator to proofread and check screen documents, but the operator must still take care to ensure the accuracy of the text.

directory Every document or file that is stored on a disk must be given a name. The document is saved under this name and displayed on a screen directory or index, which is a list of all the documents stored on a disk. Most word processing systems will display the list in alphabetical order; this is most convenient for the operator when a particular document needs to be identified and recalled to the screen.

On many systems the directory consists of nothing more than a

D I R E C T O R Y

Page 1 Press 'down' cursor arrow for next page

FILENAME	SIZE	DATE	TIME	AUTHOR
ADVERTS	10320	14-06-9-	0954	PBK
ADVERTS.BAK	8764	10-06-9-	1010	PBK
EXPENSES	536	16-07-9-	1715	PBK
PRODUCTS	1526	12-07-9-	1218	PBK
PRODUCTS.BAK	1432	10-07-9-	1115	DRM
PRICES	9005	16-07-9-	1033	RJS
SALES	1806	15-07-9-	1421	PBK
SALES.BAK	1735	14-07-9-	1335	PBK

directory

list of the documents and back-up copies (generally identified by the characters .BAK after the file name). Other systems provide the operator with additional information such as the amount of storage space occupied by the document, eg, 10 K, and the date on which it was created or last amended. These systems may also allow the operator to change the listing of the items in the directory from alphabetical to chronological order (ie date order).

discretionary hyphen (See **soft hyphen.**)

disk A circular plate, generally covered with a magnetic medium, used in computing and word processing, on which information may be stored electronically. The data is stored randomly along concentric circles called tracks. Floppy disks are made of a flexible material, housed in a stiff cover to protect the disk, and are available in various sizes. Floppy disks are 8 inches in diameter, mini-floppies 5.25 inches and micro-floppies 3.25 inches or 3.5 inches in diameter. Disks should be handled and stored with care to protect the data stored on them. (See **disk care**.) Floppy disks may be single sided or double sided (SS or DS), which means that data may be stored on one side or on both sides, and single density or double density (SD or DD), which refers to the amount of information that can be stored on the disk. Single sided, single density disks hold less data than double sided, double density disks.

Hard disks, used on larger systems or networked systems, are capable of storing vast quantities of information. Hard disks sealed in a special unit are often known as Winchester disks.

Floppy disks and hard disks are magnetic media. Laser optical disks are non-magnetic media, the data being recorded on the disk by means of tiny laser beams. (See **laser optical disk.**)

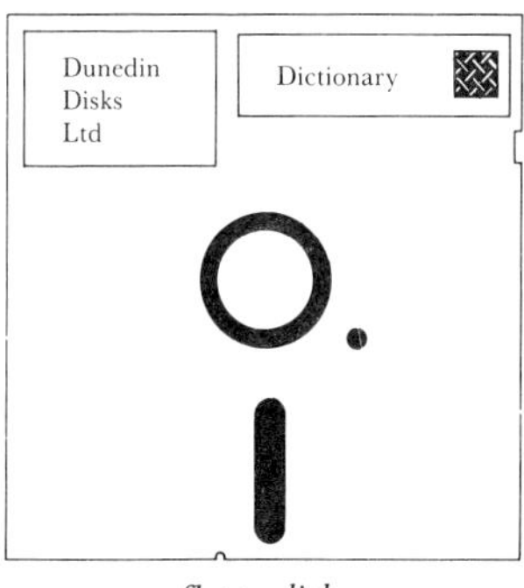

floppy disk

disk care Care should be taken of new, unused disks and of disks containing stored data. Floppy disks can be damaged very easily and the data stored on them may be lost. In order to avoid damage, keep disks dry, free from dust, away from any source of heat or any magnetic source, and take care not to touch the exposed areas of the disk. Do not bend a disk or place it on top of the VDU or printer, and never force it into the disk drive. Wait until the drive operating light switches off before removing a disk from the drive. Always replace disks in their protective envelopes after use and store them vertically in a special disk storage container or disk file. Ensure that all disks are labelled to indicate their contents. Write on the disk label before sticking it on to a disk, or use a special soft-tipped disk labelling pen. Make a security back-up copy of any disk containing important information and take care to up-date the security copy whenever the original disk is amended.

disk drive An electronic device forming part of a computer or word processing system which is used to 'write' information on to a disk and to 'read' the information that has been stored by means of a *write head* and a *read head.* Some word processors use a single drive whilst others have two drives (dual drive systems). A dual drive system is far more convenient for the operator because the system disk can be inserted into one drive while the working, or data, disk is inserted into the other. Users of a single drive system constantly have to change disks while they work.

disk operating system (DOS) The program that prepares the computer or word processor so that it is ready to accept an applications package such as a word processing program, a database or a spreadsheet program.

disk space remaining The amount of space available on a disk for storing information. You should make a habit of checking the available space on a disk whenever you use the word processor. If, when you instruct the word processor to save the file, the system responds with a message that there is insufficient space available for saving the document, you will lose the text that has been keyed in. Consider a disk to be full when there are about 25 pages left. This will allow you sufficient disk space if any of the stored documents need editing at a later date.

The amount of disk space remaining is usually found by selecting a menu option to check the disk space. The space available may be stated in terms of pages or of kilobytes free. You can increase the space available by deleting any unwanted documents or files. (See **housekeeping.**)

display The text shown on the VDU screen. On most word processors the display is 80 characters wide by 26 lines long, referred to as a half page display. Some word processors have full page displays, 80 characters wide by 68 lines long, and desktop publishing systems may have even larger display screens to help the operator manipulate the text and pictures.

Some electronic typewriters are equipped with a single line display, or 'thin window display' on a narrow strip of screen above the keyboard. The operator can see the last few words of text keyed in, and if necessary amend them before they are printed on the page.

Display also refers to the layout or presentation of text on a page, including headings, paragraph style, line spacing and various methods of emphasis. Headings may be displayed at the left margin, indented, or centred and emphasised by using closed capitals, spaced capitals, centring, underlining or emboldening. Paragraphs of text may be displayed in blocked, indented or hanging style, or as two or more columns. The whole display may be centred both horizontally and vertically on the page.

display format The manner in which text is displayed on screen. A screen display that shows the text exactly as it will be printed is the most helpful to the operator. This is often referred to as 'What You See Is What You Get' (WYSIWYG) display.

distribution copies The copies of a document which are to be sent to the individuals named on a distribution list.

distribution list A list giving the names of people to whom a copy of a document is to be sent. A separate document will be sent to each person named on the distribution list, which is typed either at the top or the bottom of the document so that everyone knows who has received a copy. (See **circulation list.**)

ditto The word ditto, meaning 'the same thing', is sometimes contracted to 'do', or represented by the double quotation mark (") . It is used where a word or section of text is repeated, particularly in handwritten documents, to save the time that would be spent in writing the word(s) again.

In typewritten or word processed documents it is often preferable to repeat the word(s) instead of using dittos. If you use a word processor you can use the copy and paste function to copy the words and paste them in where required. However, some people do prefer the dittos to be used and you should follow the author's preference. If the ditto marks (") are used, place each one in a central position below the word it refers to.

division of words Anyone using a typewriter has to make a decision as to whether a long word will fit at the end of a line or whether to return the carriage and place it on the next line. Word processors (and some electronic typewriters) are programmed to make that decision for the typist or operator by means of the automatic wordwrap function. However, the movement of a long word to the next line can, in some cases, leave a fairly large open space (known as white space) at the end of a line when a ragged right margin is used, or between words on the line when a justified right margin is used. This may not be desirable, particularly when a short line length is used.

To avoid too much white space along the line, a word may be divided into two parts. The beginning of the word is placed on one line, followed immediately by a hyphen to indicate that the word is incomplete, and the rest of the word is taken down to the next line. Many word processing systems have a hyphenation function that automatically divides the words in this way, but on some systems the operator must make the decision about where to divide the word when using the hyphenation function.

Divide a word according to its sense and sound, so that it can still be read and understood easily, eg, type- writer (*not* typewr- iter) and satis- factory or satisfac- tory (*not* satisfa- ctory). Divide hyphenated words at the hyphen.

A word consisting of a single syllable should not be divided. Numbers, dates, abbreviations and, wherever possible, names should not be divided. Make use of the protected space function (or coded, or non-breaking space) to ensure that items such as these are not divided.

document There are two types of document: screen documents and printed documents. A screen document is any text which is typed or keyed in to a word processor and which is displayed on the screen. It exists as a document whether or not it has been named or filed (stored on disk), depending on the method of naming and storing used by a particular word processing system. Once it has been saved and is listed on the directory it may be referred to as either a document or a file, again depending on the system being used or the preference of the operator.

Once text has been printed on to paper, either by using a typewriter or by printing from the word processor, it becomes a printed document.

document assembly A word processing term referring to the process of combining, or assembling, sections of text from one or more documents to produce a new document. The procedure may also be referred to as boilerplating or merging, and it may involve the use of a phrase file or a standard paragraph file.

document name Every document must be given a unique name (ie no two documents may bear exactly the same name) before it is saved on the disk, so that it can be listed on the directory and easily identified when it is necessary to recall it to the screen at a later date. A document name (or file name) should indicate the contents of the document as clearly as possible, given the number of characters available for the name. This is obviously easier if twenty-five characters can be used for a name, as compared with the eight characters available on many systems. Where only a few characters can be used for the document name, it is necessary to use abbreviations such as JUNSFIGS for JUNE SALES FIGURES.

Unfortunately you may not be able to remember what the abbreviated name means if the document has been stored for some time. Always make the name as explanatory as possible. You may also find it useful to add your initials to the document name.

Some systems do not allow certain characters or symbols to be included in a document name, eg, / : or a space. On many word processors the system automatically makes a back-up copy when a document has been recalled to the screen and filed for a second time, and this is listed on the directory under the original name, plus a full stop and the abbreviation BAK, eg, JUNSFIGS.BAK.

document recovery When a document has been deleted, either accidentally by an operator or as the result of a machine fault or program error, it is useful to be able to recover the document. Some word processors offer this facility, or it may be possible to use a special computer program disk to recover the file.

dongle A chip that must be fitted in a microcomputer to enable it to operate programs supplied by certain software manufacturers with the intention of preventing illegal copying of the programs.

dot matrix A pattern of dots formed by the printhead of a dot matrix printer to produce characters on paper. (See **printer**.)

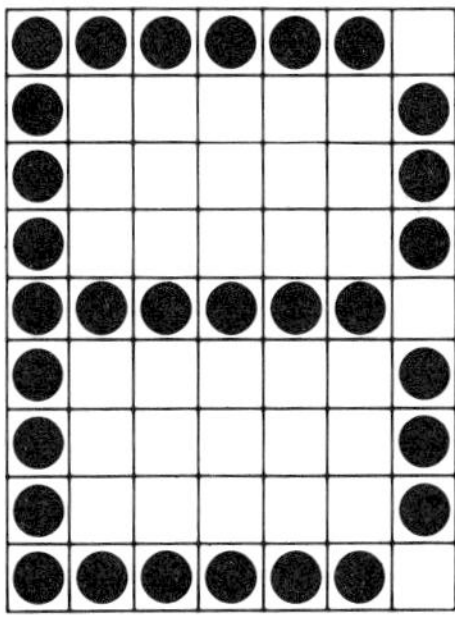

a dot matrix

dotted line A line consisting of a row of dots formed by typing a series of full stops. Dotted lines are used in forms to show the person completing the form where certain information should be inserted in ink or on the typewriter, and in this case they are often referred to as insertion lines.

Where a row of dots is used in a table to connect text with a column of figures, the dotted line is known as a leader line.

double column display The line length should be the same for each column of a double column display. When A4 paper is used with 12 pitch type, for example, the number of characters used for each column may be 35, with left and right margins of 12 and 12, plus 6 character spaces between the columns.

When a typewriter is used, set the margins at 12 and 47 and type the first column of text. Roll the paper back to the first line of type, or remove the paper from the typewriter and re-insert it, then type the second column.

If you use a word processor you may be able to type the whole of the text in one long column, the width of the first column, and use a *cut column* function to cut the lower half of the column and paste it in again at the appropriate position for the second column. If this facility is not available, you may be able to set tab stops and to type the text of each column within the space allocated for the line length.

Alternatively, you can type the whole of the text as a single column and divide it into two equal parts by inserting a *hard page break* at the appropriate point. You can then change the margins of the second page so that the column will be printed on the right-hand side of the page. You can then print the first page with the column on the left-hand side of the paper. Re-insert the paper in the printer and print the second page on the right-hand of the paper, or if you are using continuous stationery roll the paper back to the appropriate position, and print the second page, which will have the column at the right-hand side of the page.

GRIEVANCES AND DISPUTES

The Company aims at all times to operate in such a way that grievances or disputes are unlikely to arise. Supervisors, Managers and our employees are all encouraged to develop the type of business relationships that allow the full discussion and resolution of any problem the moment it arises.

If you have any queries or problems, please approach your Supervisor in the first instance. He or she will make every effort to give you full and correct answers. If your Supervisor feels it is necessary to pass the problem to a more senior Manager you will be given a date by which you will have a reply. In accordance with our grievance procedure, this date will be within five working days.

If your Supervisor's manager is confident that the problem has been settled as fully and fairly as possible in the circumstances, you will be informed of this decision, and it will be confirmed in writing within twenty-four hours.

If, however, you are still not satisfied when you receive this answer, you may ask your Supervisor to arrange a meeting with the Branch Manager for further discussion. At this stage you will be asked to put your problem in writing. This meeting with the Branch Manager must take place within ten working days of your original approach and you have the right, if you wish, to be accompanied by a colleague.

Even after this, if you are still not satisfied and you feel the need to take the matter further, you may use the approved Appeals Procedure (See Appendix A).

In addition, you are fully entitled to take advantage of any approved Union grievance procedure, provided it is as a member of one of the Unions with which the Company has an agreement.

double column display

double line heading If a heading to a column of text or figures is too wide for the column it may be split between two lines to form a double line heading. If it is split into three or more lines, it is known as a multiple line heading.

```
SINGLE LINE        DOUBLE LINE         MULTIPLE LINE
COLUMN             COLUMN              COLUMN
HEADING            HEADING             HEADING
```

Replies
4,756 3,201 2,275

Number of replies
4,756 3,201 2,275

Number of replies received
4,756 3,201 2,275

single, double and multiple line headings

down time The length of time a computer or word processor is out of action as a result of a technical fault. In business terms down time can be very costly because an expensive piece of equipment and its operator are out of action and earning no money for the business. In addition, business operations may be held up because information such as customer accounts held on the computer or word processor cannot be accessed and processed.

draft A document produced specifically for the purpose of editing by the author or by other people, so that it can be amended before the final version is produced. In some cases, such as a complicated report, the document may go through several draft versions before it is ready for the final version. Drafts are normally typed in double line spacing, with wide margins, to allow plenty of room for amendments or additions. The word DRAFT should be typed in capitals at the top of the page.

If the draft has been produced on a typewriter it will be necessary to retype the edited draft. If it has been keyed in and stored on a word processor, the operator can simply recall the document to screen and use the editing functions to amend it as required.

dummy cursor (See **ruler cursor.**)

E

editing text Documents are often prepared in draft form so that they can be read and checked by the author(s) and any necessary amendments made. The process of amending the text is known as editing. Text editing signs, also known as correction signs, are used to draw the operator's attention to words or sections of text that must be changed, inserted or deleted. In addition the author(s) of the document may wish the format of the text to be changed.

When the document has been prepared and stored on a word processor, the operator recalls it to the screen to make the changes indicated by the text editing signs. The process of amending the text is also known as editing, and the changes are made using the system's editing functions, eg insertion, deletion, cut and paste.

electronic filing Information stored on a disk, by means of a word processing program, a spreadsheet or a database program, is said to be electronically filed. The main aim in electronic filing is to store as much data as possible in such a way that it can be accessed and retrieved easily, speedily and accurately.

electronic mail Documents produced on one word processor (or computer) can be transmitted electronically to a large mainframe computer, which passes the message simultaneously to one or more receiving terminals (word processors or computers).

The originator of the message creates a specially formatted document with mail-sending software. The electronic message consists of two parts: the envelope, ie the address details, and the contents. The contents include the header, consisting of the subject heading and the time the message was sent, and the body, which contains the information of the message.

A message may be given despatch priority status, such as Very Urgent, Urgent, Standard, or Overnight. A *store and forward* facility may be used to send a message to a switching centre where it can be stored temporarily until the appropriate time for it to be forwarded to its destination. This helps to overcome the problem of time zone differences in other countries, and it allows messages to be stored until cheaper-rate call charges are available.

When it arrives at the receiving terminal(s) it may be stored until the user is ready to access and read it. The terminal displays a message informing the user that mail is waiting to be brought to the screen and read. If necessary, the message can be printed out at the recipient's terminal.

The term electronic mail also includes other forms of electronic message transfer such as facsimile systems (FAX) and telex.

electronic mailbox An electronic receiving station (similar to a post-office box) to which a message can be sent and where the message remains until it is collected by the addressee calling it up on his/her computer. Each user has a personal 'call sign' or number to ensure that messages left in the mailbox can be accessed only by authorised persons.

electronic message Any message (document) sent from one destination and received at another destination through electronic means, ie, a message prepared and transmitted from one computer terminal and received by another computer.

electronic office The theoretical ideal of an office in which everything possible is carried out electronically by means of computerised office systems. In the electronic office all messages would be keyed into a computer, despatched electronically, and received at other computer terminals. All documents, both internal and external, would be originated, despatched, filed, processed and retrieved electronically.

There would be no need for paper copies of any documents, giving rise to the term 'the paperless office'. Although office systems have not yet reached the fully fledged electronic office stage, there has been some movement towards it.

elision The contraction of words by omitting letters, such as the omission of the letter *o* from the word *not*, resulting in words such as *wouldn't, can't* or *didn't*, used in writing to express the way in which people speak. A single quotation mark is inserted to show that a letter has been omitted.

elite A size of type. In typewriting elite type measures twelve character spaces to one inch.

ellipsis The omission of words when quoting from another source, eg, 'and fifty per cent . . . were of the opinion that . . . all health risks had been taken into account'. Three spaced, or unspaced, full stops are inserted to show that text has been omitted.

embedded code Coded characters used on some word processing systems to send commands to the printer in connection with the text. The characters ^B may be placed at each end of a section of text that is to be emboldened, and the characters ^U may be used to indicate that the text should be underlined. The text will therefore appear on the screen as ^B ^U This is a Heading ^B ^U. When the text is printed the embedded command codes will not be printed, but the text will appear emboldened and underlined, eg, **This is a Heading.** It is usually possible to suppress the embedded codes on the screen to make proofreading and checking easier.

emboldening Sections of text, such as headings, may be highlighted to draw the reader's attention by the use of the emboldening function on a word processor or electronic typewriter. Each character is printed twice, the second time fractionally to the right of the first time, so that the character appears much blacker than the normal print. Emboldening is also referred to as bold print.

enclosures An enclosure is any document, such as an advertising leaflet, report, etc, placed in an envelope with a letter (ie, enclosed with the letter).It is usual to alert the reader to the presence of an enclosure by typing the word 'Enclosure(s)' at the left-hand margin, two or three clear line spaces below the complimentary close of the letter. Alternatively, 'Enc', 'Encs' or 'Att' (for attached) may be typed to indicate the presence of an enclosure. Some people like to type three full stops within the left margin at the point where an enclosure is mentioned in the text.

When the mail is opened, the person opening the letter should check to ensure that any enclosure indicated has, in fact, been included with the letter.

encryption A term meaning the purposeful distortion of messages sent by electronic mail, in order to prevent unauthorised people from having access to the information held in the message. The sender passes the message through a 'scrambling' machine before despatching it and the addressee has a de-scrambler through which the message is passed before it can be read.

The encryption of data has two main purposes: to prevent the unauthorised disclosure of information, and to prevent the unauthorised modification of information.

end of text marker Some word processors display a marker symbol on the screen to indicate the end of the text. Other systems display the words 'END OF TEXT'. The cursor must be positioned to the left of the end of text marker when you wish to key in text.

entry point The point at which any text will be entered when a character is pressed on the keyboard, as indicated by the position at which the cursor is resting.

enumeration A list of items in order, numbered with arabic or roman numerals, or with letters of the alphabet.

envelope A sealable wrapping for letters, on which the name and address of the recipient may be written or typed. The sender's name and address should also be written, typed, printed or stamped on the envelope, preferably on the reverse side, as a 'return address' in case the Post Office is unable to deliver the letter.

There are many types and sizes of envelopes. The most commonly used envelopes include the 'banker', which opens along one long side, the 'pocket', which opens at one of the shorter ends, and the 'window', which incorporates a transparent window allowing the address typed on a suitably folded letter to be used as the address for postal purposes. An aperture envelope is similar to a window envelope, but the cut-out address panel is not covered with transparent material. Window and aperture envelopes save time, as the name and address do not have to be typed on the envelope.

The envelope sizes most commonly used for letters are the DL, which will take a sheet of A4 paper folded twice, C4, C5 and C6. These envelope sizes are illustrated here, showing how the paper should be folded to fit into them.

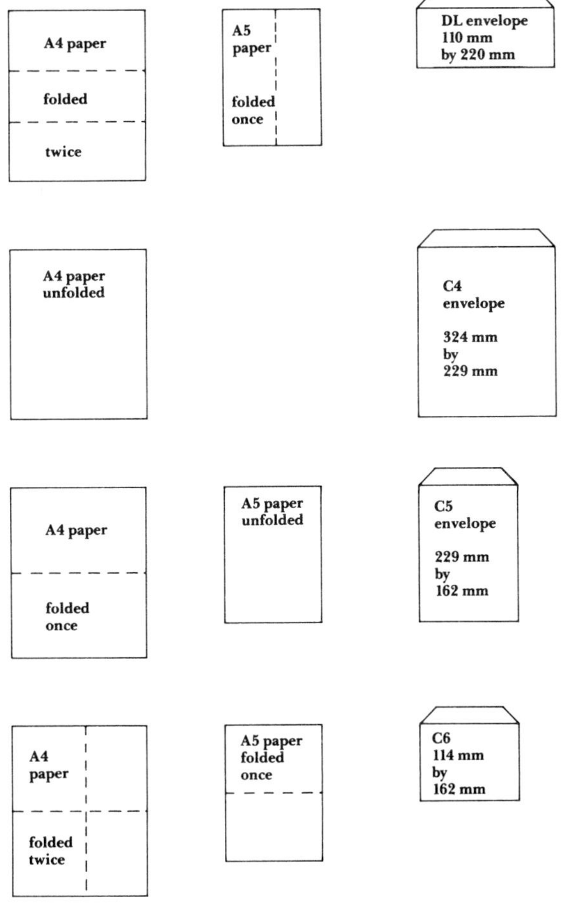

envelope sizes

Envelopes are available in various types of material, including paper, paper reinforced with card or plastic bubble material, indestructible material which cannot be torn, clear polythene and card. Take care to select an envelope of the most appropriate size, quality and material for the item(s) it is to contain.

ergonomics The study of people within, and in relation to, their working environment, with the intention of improving working conditions to produce maximum working efficiency. The study of ergonomics is concerned with the design of equipment, software, furniture and environmental conditions in order to improve factors affecting health, job satisfaction, efficiency, comfort and safety.

erratum note A short message accompanying a document or inserted into a book, alerting the reader to the fact that one or more errors appear in the document or book.

error message A message displayed on the screen of a word processor or computer when an incorrect command is given to the system by the operator. Error messages appear at either the top or bottom of the screen in what is known as a prompt line area. Some systems will identify the precise error that has been made, whilst others will simply state that an error has been made.

escape key A dedicated key that, on many word processing systems, allows the operator to leave the current document temporarily, and to return to it by pressing the escape key a second time.

execute (exec) A command given to a word processor to carry out (or execute) the instructions it has been given by pressing the appropriate key sequence.

execute key A dedicated key that enters a command into the word processor. This function may also be carried out by the enter key or the return key. Instructions, or commands, are given to the system by pressing the appropriate key(s) for a given function, such as centring or emboldening. The command will not, however, be carried out until the execute, enter or return key has been pressed.

exit An option that may be chosen by a word processing operator from a list of menu options in order to leave (or exit from) the word processing program and return to the operating system. The term may also be used to describe the leaving of a document in order to print or work on another document. The term *quit* may be used for the same function on some systems.

external memory A long-term or permanent memory device, other than the main memory, for storage of computer/word processing programs, data or text, eg, a disk or magnetic tape.

external storage Any storage medium, eg, disk or tape, that can be removed from the word processing system and stored somewhere else.

F

facsimile (FAX) Electronic mailing equipment that scans a document and transmits it electronically at high speeds to a location anywhere in the world, where the receiving terminal accepts it and prints it on paper. The paper may be in the form of a large roll so that the receiving Fax terminal can automatically receive a number of transmitted documents, one after the other, print each message, cut the paper to length and stack it, without the need for an operator in attendance. This is useful if messages are to be received overnight. One of the main advantages of Fax systems is that printed, typewritten or handwritten text, diagrams, plans or photographs can be transmitted. (See **electronic mail.**)

fanfold Continuous printer stationery is perforated at the appropriate length for a page and folded along the perforations into a stack that can be opened up like a fan. On each side of the paper is a perforated strip punched with sprocket holes to fit the tractor feed mechanism of the printer. The fanfolding and sprocket holes permit easy feeding into and through the printer, and automatic stacking as the printed pages are fed out of the printer. The paper may then be torn or guillotined into page lengths and the perforated side strips removed.

FAX (See **facsimile**.)

field A sorting category used for processing data stored in a records file or database. Each field consists of a single piece of information (such as a name, date, or address) stored in a data file or database. The data in a field may be a number, a word or several words.

field name Each field in a data file or database is given a field name as an identifier. This is usually in an abbreviated form, eg: SNME for surname, ADDR for address or PCDE for postcode. The field names are used when instructing the computer to sort or select particular fields from the data file, or to merge them with a standard document. The example below shows a record containing six field names with the field values (ie, the data) printed alongside.

```
FNME Keith            STNO 4475
SNME Derbyshire       JOB  Purchasing Manager
DEPT Purchasing       GRDE Grade VI
```

field names

figures (See **numbers.**)

file A folder in which are kept paper documents, usually all related to a specific topic area. Each file should be labelled with an appropriate name. A collection of files may be kept in a filing cabinet, and stored according to a logical system such as alphabetical, subject or numerical filing.

In word processing the term 'file' may be used as an alternative to the word 'document'. Word processing files are stored on disk, and they are listed by name on the system's index, or directory. Depending on which word processing program is used, they may be listed randomly or alphabetically.

file copy A copy of a document stored in a file as a record and for future reference purposes. Paper file copies may be produced by using carbon paper, by photocopying the master copy or by printing an additional copy, and they will be stored in a filing cabinet. In some organisations file copies of documents may be stored on disk instead of in the form of a paper copy. A file copy should always be kept of all business correspondence and most other business documents. (See **carbon copy.**)

file name The identifying name given to a file should be easily recognisable and should describe the information held in the file, whether it is a paper or card file, or a word processed document. (See **document name.**)

flag symbols Characters that may appear on the VDU screen to indicate the presence of, for example, a hard return or a line that extends beyond the right-hand side of the screen. Although these characters appear on the screen, they are not printed when the text is printed out.

flow chart A pictorial representation of tasks or operations, listed in sequential order, which must be carried out to obtain a particular objective. Specific symbols and shapes are used, such as circles, diamonds and rectangles. Information is written inside and outside the symbols, to denote the start or finish of an operation, data to be input, processed, output and so on. The symbols are joined by lines marked with arrows to show the direction of 'flow' (sequential movement) within the chart.

Flow charts are used during the preparation stages of writing programs for computers, and in the analysis and structuring of physical operations such as the flow of paper documents through a company or the procedures to be followed in the production of a manufactured article. (See page 51.)

flow lines Lines drawn between symbols in a flow chart or organisation chart. Arrow heads drawn on the lines indicate the direction of flow or movement through the chart.

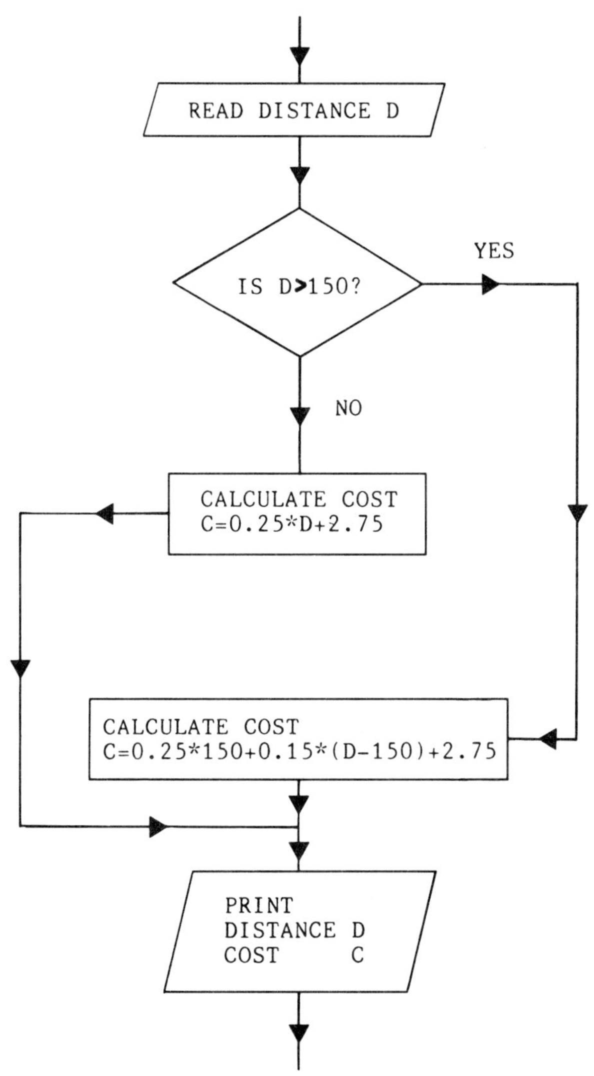
READ DISTANCE D
IS D>150?
YES
NO
CALCULATE COST
C=0.25*D+2.75
CALCULATE COST
C=0.25*150+0.15*(D-150)+2.75
PRINT
DISTANCE D
COST C

flow chart

flush left Text that is printed (or displayed on the VDU screen) with the left-hand margin lined up vertically but with a ragged right margin. (See **justification.**)

flush right Text that is printed (or displayed on the VDU screen) with the right-hand margin lined up vertically but with a ragged left margin. (See **justification.**)

folded screen When a wide document (ie one that is wider than the screen display) is being prepared on the word processor, the operator cannot view the full line of the document because the screen is not wide enough. On most systems it is necessary to use horizontal scrolling to move the document from side to side so that the full line can be read.

If it is necessary to compare data on the left of the document with data on the right, eg, columns of figures, it is possible on some systems to 'fold' the screen display. The display is split, and a vertical window on the right-hand side of the screen displays text or figures from the right-hand side of the document, as if a piece of paper were folded over.

font A character set of given size, style and typeface containing lower-case and upper-case characters, numbers, punctuation marks and symbols such as £, $ and @. The font may be changed on a daisywheel printer by changing the daisywheel printhead. When a dot matrix, ink jet or laser printer is used, a wide variety of fonts is available to the operator. (See **character set**.)

footer Information keyed into the footer space of a screen document that is automatically printed within the bottom margin of every page, or of selected pages of a document. This is sometimes referred to as a running footer. Footer details are not usually printed on the first page of a document.

Footer information generally consists of details such as the page number, a reference code and/or the word *Continued* . . . . Footer details, once keyed in, may be edited or deleted in the same ways as text in the main part of the document. (See **header.**)

footer space A space at the bottom of a screen document that represents the bottom margin when the document is printed. Information keyed into the footer space is automatically printed on every page or on selected pages. (See **footer**.) The number of line spaces available in the footer space may be reduced or increased, and obviously this affects the number of line spaces available on the page for the main body of the text.

footnote Supplementary information that is placed at the bottom of a page to avoid disruption of the flow of text, eg, in a particular paragraph the author may refer to a book from which details were taken. The title, author, publisher and any other necessary information may be typed at the bottom of the page in the form of a footnote.

A superscripted symbol or number is typed at the point of reference to indicate that further information is shown at the bottom of the page. The same symbol or reference number is typed at the beginning of the footnote. In many documents the modern practice is to collect together all references for a chapter, or a section of a report, and to print them at the end of that chapter or section.

Footnotes should be typed in single line spacing, with a clear line space between separate footnotes, whatever line spacing is used for the main body of the text. The symbol or number should be typed close up to the appropriate reference word in the text, but a space should be left between the symbol or number and the footnote at the bottom of the page.

A continuous underscored line is often typed from margin to margin to separate footnotes from the text in a document such as a report, article or book. However, footnotes are often used in tables or forms, and no separating line is necessary on this type of document.

Some word processors have a footnote function that automatically numbers each footnote. This also ensures that footnotes always appear on the page on which they are referred to, or that they are automatically collected together and printed on the last page of the document. The footnote function may also allow the operator to choose whether a separating line is required between the text and the footnote.

The time taken by Central Office Services to produce documents has been reduced significantly since the introduction of job control procedures[1] last year. However, it is hoped that the introduction of bonus payments will increase productivity still further and the Department is currently analysing its data on this project.[2] The proposal has the support of the Unions and of the majority of employees in Central Office Services.

---

1 This was the subject of a special report: "Job Control and Analysis in the Production of Documents".

2 A report on the likely effects of introducing bonus payments will be submitted to the next Board meeting.

footnotes to text

STAFFING LEVELS*

SECTION	CURRENT STAFFING	PROPOSED STAFFING
Secretarial	27	23
WP Operators	32	29
Clerical	15	12
Supervisory	5	3
Training	-	1**

* These figures do not take into account the employment of temporary staff to cover maternity leave, etc.

** One of the present Supervisors could be transferred to this role, after an appropriate training course.

footnotes to tables

footprint The area of a desk that is occupied by a word processor or microcomputer.

foreground printing Printing of text displayed on the screen, ie the text is not necessarily stored.

form A page of text, displayed on a VDU screen or printed on paper, presenting questions or requesting information in a standard format with spaces for the answers to be filled in by the person responding to the form. Spaces for information on a printed form may be identified by solid or dotted lines (known as insertion lines), boxes or blank spaces. Blank spaces are left on screen forms, which may have insertion points identified by markers or symbols.

format The layout of text on a page or on the VDU screen, including the size of the margins, the type of margin (left or right aligned, or justified), single or double column display, centring or other enhancement of headings, the line spacing and the font used. The format may be set through the menu of a word processor or by inserting information on a format line on the screen of the VDU.

format saving If a particular format is used for documents that are frequently prepared, such as memos, letters, reports or financial statements, the format may be prepared and saved on a master document. This saves the time and effort involved in setting the format each time a document is prepared. The document containing the saved format may be duplicated or copied when a new memo, letter, etc, is to be typed.

format setting A format for the display of text is entered into a word processing program by the programmer. This format, known as the default format or default setting, is automatically used unless the operator enters new format settings.

formatting disks Also referred to as initialising. Most unused floppy disks need to be prepared for use on the word processor or computer by carrying out a procedure known as formatting or initialising. A program disk is placed in one disk drive and the new disk in the other disk drive, and a command to format or initialise is given. The program disk checks the alignment of the sectors on the disk to ensure that the disk can be aligned with the heads in the disk drive. The process generally includes allocation of a name to the disk so that it can be identified by the computer whenever it is inserted in a disk drive. For many systems it is possible to buy pre-formatted disks.

form design The way in which information is displayed on a form. Forms to be completed on a typewriter should conform to the standard six lines to one inch of vertical depth so that the typist does not have to adjust the line spacing for each answer.

form letter A standard letter prepared with spaces for the insertion of variable information, such as the date, the recipient's name and address and the salutation. The letter is designed so that it can be sent to a large number of people with the minimum number of changes to the text.

When a typewriter is used, the variable details are typed on photocopied or printed copies of the letter. In preparing the form letter, therefore, it is necessary to leave sufficient space at the insertion points for the variable information to be typed in.

When a word processor is used it is not necessary to leave spaces, but easily identifiable symbols must be typed at the insertion points. The variable details may be inserted by the operator, or where appropriate the merge function can be used to select the appropriate variable details from a records file and automatically merge them with the form letter.

Form letters are also referred to as skeleton letters.

fractions Some keyboards are provided with keys for fractions such as ¼, ½ and ¾. If special keys are not available on the keyboard, fractions may be typed as sloping fractions, eg, 5/8, 2/3 or 3/4. If a number includes both whole numbers and fractions, leave a space between the two parts, eg, 3 1/4, 4 1/2 or 3 3/4. Alternatively the fraction may be expressed as 3.25, 4.5 or 3.75.

friction feed The part of a printer that feeds single sheets of paper into the machine from the cassette or hopper that holds the paper supply.

function Any word processing operation such as centre, embolden, cut and paste or search and replace.

function keys Keys on the keyboard of an electronic typewriter or word processor that carry out a given task, such as centre, undo, superscript or embolden. The function to which the key is dedicated is printed on the surface of the key. Also known as dedicated function keys or control keys.

G

gateway A telecommunications device used to interface networks so that a computer terminal on one network can communicate with a computer terminal on another network.

glossary A list of frequently used words or phrases prepared by a word processor operator and stored on disk as a document, along with identifier codes. The stored words or terms may be automatically recalled and inserted into another document when required. This saves time in typing and proofreading frequently used words that are difficult to spell, particularly in specialist fields such as medicine or in technical industries.

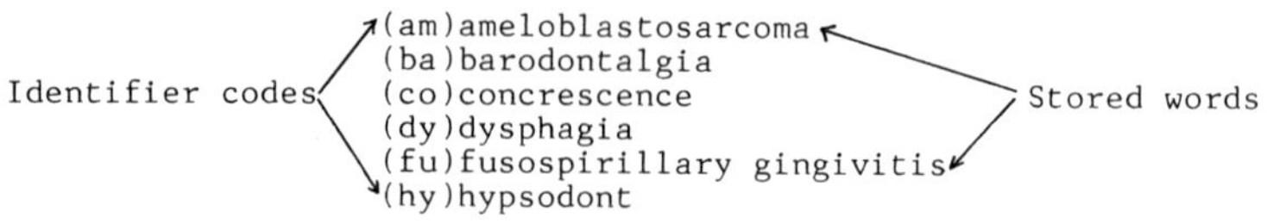

glossary

graph A diagram representing a relationship between two or more variables (also known as a chart). Among the many types of graph are: line graphs, in which data points are connected by a single line; bar or column charts, in which data is presented as separate bars or columns; pie charts, in which data is represented as segments of a circle, one or more of the segments being withdrawn from the circle in an exploded pie chart.

graphics Some word processors have a line drawing graphics facility that allows the operator to produce horizontal and vertical lines on screen and on the printout. This facility is useful for drawing a box around text or in the production of flow charts.

A variety of computer programs are available that allow the operator to produce graphs, charts, diagrams or detailed drawings on a computer and these are known as graphics programs. Integrated programs permit the operator to select diagrams or pictures from the graphics program and insert them into a word processed document.

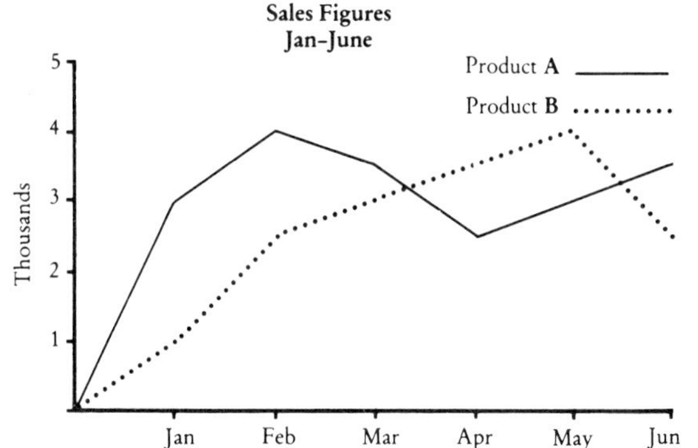
Sales Figures
Jan–June
Product A
Product B
Thousands
5
4
3
2
1
Jan
Feb
Mar
Apr
May
Jun
Line
Graph

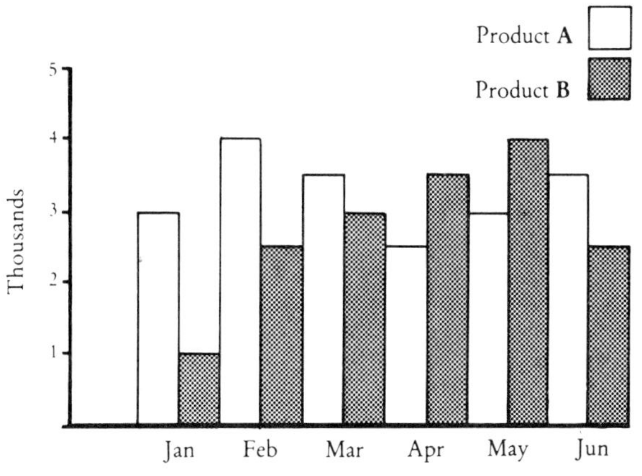
Product A
Product B
Thousands
5
4
3
2
1
Jan
Feb
Mar
Apr
May
Jun
Column
Chart

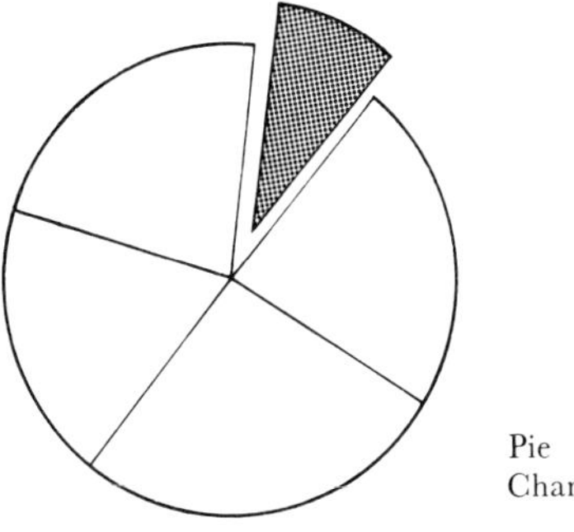
Pie
Chart

types of graph

graphic tablet A peripheral input device that may be used in addition to, or instead of, the keyboard for inputting data into a computer program or word processing program.

guide keys The eight keys on the middle row of the charater keys on a keyboard, over which the fingers of both hands hover ready to reach for, and press, any key on the keyboard. The guide keys on the QWERTY keyboard are ASDF and JKL;. Also referred to as the home keys.

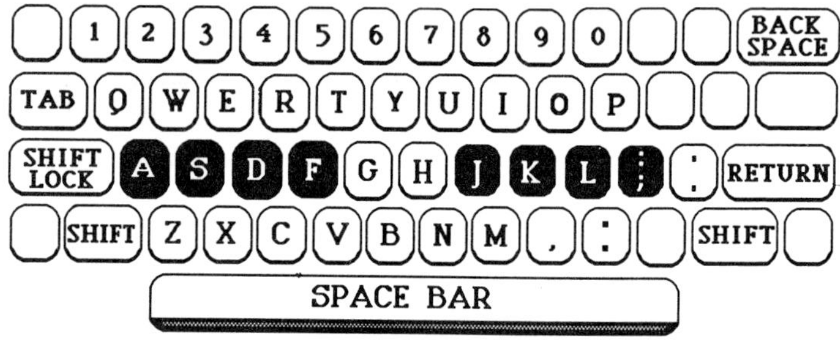

guide keys

H

hacker An individual who makes unauthorised access to data stored on a computer or in an electronic mailbox, either to read it, amend it or use it illegally, for example by transferring funds.

handshake A term used in data communications to describe the process of exchanging signals when a connection is made across an interface between computer equipment to ensure that it is working correctly.

hard copy Word processing or computer output in the form of print on paper. (See **soft copy**.)

hard hyphen A word processing term describing the insertion of a hyphen into a word or between words by the operator, eg, the hyphens in *day-to-day* are always required and should be keyed in with the hyphen key. A hard hyphen will remain in the word no matter where the word is moved to on a line of text when editing changes are made, as compared with a soft hyphen inserted by the system to indicate the division of a word at the end of a line. A hard hyphen may be removed by means of the delete function. (See **soft hyphen**.)

hard page break A page break inserted by the operator to end a page of text before the point where the soft page break would automatically be inserted by the word processing system. A hard page break may be deleted when it is no longer required. (See **soft page break**.)

hard return A word processing term referring to the insertion of a return at the end of a heading, line of text or the end of a paragraph. It is an instruction to the word processor to move the cursor, and the entry point, on to the next line. A hard return remains in the text until a command is given for it to be removed. A flag symbol may be displayed on the screen to indicate the presence of the hard return.

hard space A space inserted in text by use of the space bar, as compared with the additional 'soft' spaces that are inserted automatically by the word processing program when a line of text is justified.

hardware Pieces of equipment which make up a word processor or computer system. The major items of hardware are the visual display unit (VDU), the keyboard, the disk drives, the central processing unit and the printer.

hash sign The symbol # provided on electronic keyboards.

head The device contained in a word processor disk drive that can read, record or erase data on a magnetic disk.

headed paper Paper that has been pre-printed with the name, address and telephone number of a person, organisation or business, together with other relevant business information such as a VAT number, telex and facsimile numbers.

header Information keyed into the header space of a screen document that is automatically printed within the top margin of every page, or of selected pages of a document. This is sometimes referred to as a running header. Header details are not usually printed on the first page of a document.

Header information generally consists of details such as the title of a report or other document, a page number, the date and/or a reference code. Header details, once keyed in, may be edited or deleted in the same way as text in the main part of the document. (See **footer**).

header space A space at the top of a screen document that represents the top margin when the document is printed. Information keyed into the header space is automatically printed on every page, or on selected pages. (See **header**.) The number of line spaces available in the header space may be reduced or increased, and obviously this affects the number of line spaces available on the page for the main body of the text.

heading A single word or several words used to indicate the content of the main body of the text of a document. A main heading generally indicates what is contained in the whole document. A sub-heading summarises the contents of a section of a document. Headings may be centred over the body of the work or blocked at the left margin. Emphasis may be given to headings by the use of capitals, spaced capitals, underlining and/or emboldening.

There are various types of heading. Marginal, or side, headings occupy a column of their own at the left-hand side of the page, all text of the associated paragraphs being typed in a wider column at the right-hand side of the page. Paragraph headings start on the same line as the first line of the paragraph. Shoulder headings are blocked at the left margin, with a clear line space between the heading and the paragraph of associated text.

Vertical headings are generally used in tables to save space. When a typewriter is used the table is typed, leaving sufficient space for the vertical headings to be inserted later. The paper is removed from the typewriter and re-inserted sideways so that the headings can be typed. When a word processor is used vertical headings are typed by keying in one character per line, one below the other.

MARGINAL HEADINGS	This is a an example of a marginal, or side, heading, in which the headings occupy a separate column at the left of the text.

PARAGRAPH HEADING This is an example of a paragraph heading, in which the heading starts on the same line as the first line of the text of the paragraph.

SHOULDER HEADING

This example illustrates a shoulder heading, which is blocked at the left margin, one clear line space above the text.

THE EXAMPLE BELOW ILLUSTRATES TWO TYPES OF VERTICAL HEADING

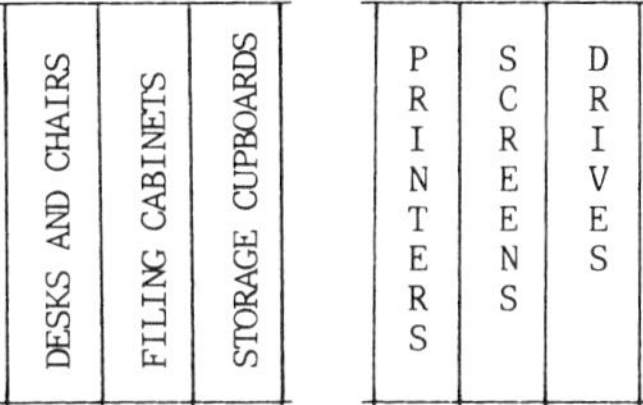

THE EXAMPLE BELOW SHOWS OBLIQUE HEADINGS

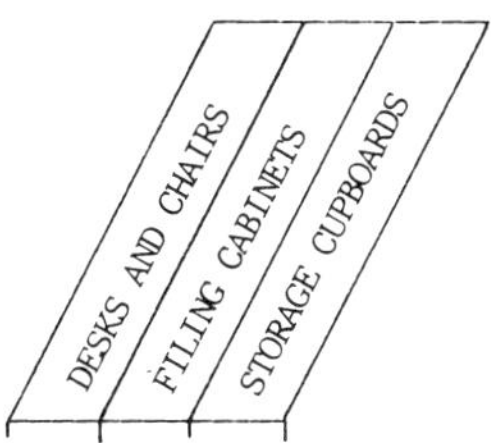

types of heading

Oblique or diagonal headings are similar to vertical headings but the headings are placed at an angle of about 45°. The table is typed, leaving sufficient space for the later insertion of the headings. The paper is removed and re-inserted into the typewriter at the desired angle so that the headings can be typed. Diagonal headings cannot be produced on a word processor.

health and safety The *Health and Safety at Work Act (1974)* placed the responsibility for health and safety at work on everyone in the workplace. Employers must conform to certain regulations such as ensuring that the building is safe, that there are adequate exits for rapid escape from the building in an emergency, that adequate protective clothing is supplied, that all machinery complies with safety regulations and so on.

The employee is responsible for complying with safety regulations such as wearing protective clothing supplied, correct handling of equipment, reporting of damaged equipment or unsafe working practices, etc. Everyone working in an office, a shop or factory should be familiar with the main provisions of the *Health and Safety at Work Act* and with the health and safety policy established at their place of work.

help file A summary of instructions for using a word processor, held on the program disk for quick reference when using the system. A help file is very useful for new users. It may be called to the screen while the operator is keying in or editing a document by pressing a special function key, or typing in a special key sequence. In effect, a help file is a shortened, screen-based version of the user manual.

highlighting The reversal of the text colour and the screen colour to identify sections of text on which word processing operations are to be carried out. Black characters on a white screen, for example, are changed to white characters on a black screen, and the operator can see clearly whether the appropriate section of text has been identified. The highlighting is automatically removed immediately the command is given to execute the function by pressing the return key or enter key. (See **reverse video**.)

home key A cursor control key that automatically returns the cursor to line one, column one, at the top left-hand corner of the VDU screen on the first page of a screen document, ie the home position.

hopper feed A cassette tray system attached to a word processor printer that allows a single sheet of paper at a time to be fed into the machine at the correct position for printing. (See **sheet feeder**.)

hotline An emergency telephone service offered by some software companies and software distributors offering the purchaser of a word processing program the opportunity to obtain rapid assistance in solving problems or seeking advice about using the program. There is usually a charge for the hotline service.

hot zone The area of about ten to fifteen character spaces at the end of a line of text on a word processor equivalent to the bell zone on a typewriter. When the text being keyed in nears the end of the line, the word processor automatically makes a decision about whether a word will fit on to the line or whether it should be moved on to the beginning of the next line through the wraparound, or wordwrap, function.

housekeeping The day-to-day organisation and/or protection of documents saved on disk on a word processor. Procedures involved in housekeeping include: logical storage of documents on disk by suitable allocation of file names; deletion of documents no longer required; duplication or copying of documents and disks; labelling of disks to indicate what has been stored on them; their storage away from computers/word processors or any magnetic field generated by other electrical equipment such as telephones; and the storage of disks in a fireproof safe when they are not in use, following a logical filing system.

house style A set of rules laid down by the management of a particular organisation for the format and layout of letters and other documents. Some businesses prepare a house style manual illustrating the layout to be followed, a copy of which is issued to every person likely to be involved with the preparation of letters or documents. House style also refers to the total image presented by the company, including the colours used for company vehicles, the logo and the typeface used for the company's name.

hyphenation The process of dividing a word into two parts if it cannot be fitted on to the current line, the first part of the word being followed by a hyphen to indicate that it is uncompleted. Word processing systems may offer an automatic hyphenation function, or an operator-assisted hyphenation function.

I

icon A small drawing displayed on a word processor screen to represent a file, a command or an operation (such as dumping unwanted files into a waste bin to delete them). Icons are also used in some word processing manuals and reference books for rapid reference to instructions for particular pieces of equipment, eg, a picture of a typewriter or word processor may be used to direct the reader's attention to the appropriate section of text for instructions.

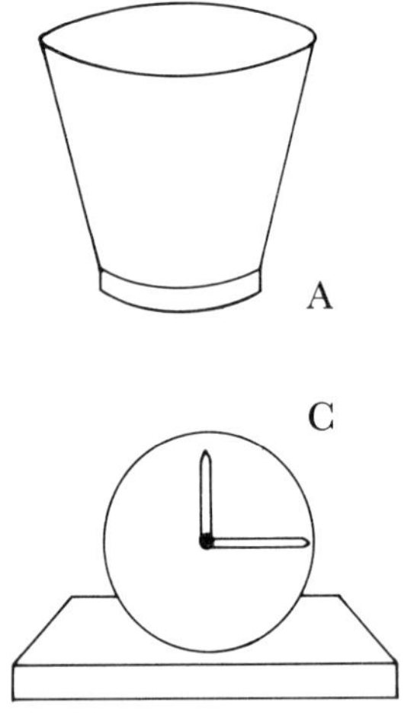

icons

(A) Waste Paper Basket – represents the 'throwing' away of documents.

(B) A Page of Text – representing word processing.

(C) A Clock – indicating that you should wait for a screen instruction before continuing.

(D) A Typewriter – indicating that the information contained in the following paragraph(s) relates to a typewriter only.

impact printer A printer which prints characters on paper by means of a mechanical impact. A type bar or the character at the end of one spoke of a daisy wheel is struck against a carbon or fabric ribbon so that the character is impressed on the paper. (See **printer**.)

image input Diagrams and other illustrative media may be copied into a computer by using a special electronic scanning device, together with an appropriate program. Once the illustration has been accepted by the computer it may be modified, saved and printed. Images input into a computer graphics program may be transferred into a word processing document or a desktop publishing program document and placed within or alongside sections of text.

incremental space The automatic insertion of variable size spaces along a line of text when using a justified right margin on an electronic typewriter or word processor, to distribute words evenly along the line without inserting large areas of white space.

indent Indentation is the positioning of text a given number of character spaces in from the left and/or right margins. The space bar may be used to move the printing point to the required position or the tabulator key may be used to move the printing point to a preset tab stop position. When a word processor is used, a new ruler line may be inserted, with the margins set at least five spaces in from the main body of the text, or the indent function may be used where this is available.

indent function The indent function is used to inset text from the left and/or the right margin.

index An organised list of the contents of a book, report, etc, together with page numbers, or of the contents of a disk showing the file names of documents stored on the disk. (See **directory**.)

indexing The process of sorting a list into a logical order by use of a range of classification activities, such as alphabetical, chronological or numerical sorting.

inferior character (See **subscript**.)

information processing In simple terms information processing can be seen as the collection and storage of information, or data, so that it may be accessed, read, amended or added to and (if desired) printed. The processed data can then be passed on to the next stage of the information processing cycle in order to provide management information on which decisions can be based. The data may be in the form of numbers, text or images, and the processing is carried out by using a computer system. Word processing, spreadsheets, databases, graphics and communications programs all come under the umbrella of information processing.

information technology In the broader sense this is the manner by which data is collected, stored, manipulated, output and interpreted by computers in commerce, industry and everyday life. It can be seen as referring to the equipment (ie the technology) used for information processing.

in-house Work carried out within a company or other organisation instead of being carried out by a specialist company. The term is often used when referring to in-house printing using desktop publishing systems instead of using a design and typesetting company.

initialisation (See **formatting disks**.)

input The insertion of text or other data into a word processor or computer by means of an input device such as a keyboard, optical character reader, mouse, touch screen, etc.

input device Equipment that allows information to be entered into the memory of a computer or word processor. Input devices include: keyboard, optical character reader, mouse, trackball, touch screen, voice input, graphics tablet and light pen. Information may also be entered into a word processor or computer directly from another terminal, as when electronic mail is transmitted.

insertion The placing of characters, words or paragraphs within the existing text of a word processing document. The word processor must be in insert mode to be able to carry out this operation. On some word processing systems it is necessary to reformat the text after inserting text.

insert mode A word processing term meaning that the computer has been given an instruction which will allow text to be input (inserted) anywhere on the blank screen or within existing text. The insertion of characters within existing text results in that text moving along the line to allow the new characters to be inserted. Most word processors have the insert mode as the default setting so that the system is always in this mode unless instructed to change to some other mode.

insetting The incorporation of text or tables within the body of a document, indented from the left and right margins. Inset items should be indented five or more character spaces from the left and right margins.

inside address The name and address of the recipient of a letter, also known as the addressee details. The inside address is usually typed between the date and the salutation on a business letter. On an informal business letter the inside address may alternatively be typed below the signature space.

integrated software A suite of computer programs that can interact with each other. Integrated programs generally consist of a combination of three or more of the following: word processing, spreadsheet, database, business presentation graphics, art graphics and communications. The purpose of the integration of software is to allow data to be transferred from one program to another. A graph or chart may, for example, be constructed from data contained in a spreadsheet program and then transferred into a word processed document.

interactive A system that involves a type of dialogue between the operator and the program in the form of questions or prompts that must be answered or responded to by the operator to ensure that a command sequence is put into operation.

interliner A lever on a typewriter that releases the platen or roller from the line space ratchet. This allows the platen to be adjusted by a fraction of a line space. The interliner is useful when it is necessary to type subscripted and superscripted characters (inferior and superior characters) or to re-align the typing point when the paper is re-inserted into the typewriter to make amendments or additions to the text.

inverse video Reversal of the screen background and text colours. If, for example, the background colour of the screen is white and the characters are black, the characters become white and the background black when in inverse video. Also known as reverse video. (See **highlighting**.)

italic A typeface that slopes slightly to the right, used to highlight words. When documents are being prepared for publication and printing, words to be printed in italics are indicated in the text by underlining.

This is a sample of an italic typeface. It may be used for informal documents such as personal letters, menus or notices. Alternatively it may be used to highlight specific words in a section of text, as shown in the example below.

In his newly-published book *The Tintinnabulus Tree*, Johannes Voight displays an exceptional understanding of the *Code of Chivalry* and its effects on the social conditions of the time.

italic script

itinerary A plan of a journey or a day's activities. A detailed itinerary is generally typed on A4 paper, with full details of the journey, timings, method of transport, hotels, meetings and social activities. A brief reminder itinerary, giving the main details of the trip, may be prepared on a postcard and kept in the traveller's pocket or handbag for quick, easy reference.

ITINERARY FOR TOUR OF EASTERN ZONE FACILITIES

Monday, 12 July, to Thursday, 15 July 199-

Transport: Company Helicopter

Monday, 12 July

0740 hours	DEPART	Head Office Helipad
0845 hours	ARRIVE	Norwich Branch Office Helipad
		All day spent touring Norwich Branch Office with Mr Joe Jurey.
2000 hours		Dinner with Mr and Mrs Jurey at their home. Mr Jurey will pick you up at the hotel.
		Overnight accommodation and breakfast at the Comcoriel Hotel, Hampton Street, Norwich, from Monday night to Wednesday night.

Tuesday, 13 July

0830 hours	DEPART	Norwich Branch Office Helipad
0950 hours	ARRIVE	Brandergast Rig Helipad.
		All day spent touring the Brandergast Rig with Mr Cy Brixtowe.
2000 hours		Dinner with Mr Brixtowe, Mr Jurey and Mr B Fazala at the Comcoriel Hotel.

Wednesday, 14 July

0830 hours	DEPART	Norwich Branch Office Helipad.
0855 hours	ARRIVE	Belsea Terminal Helipad.
		All day spent touring the Belsea Terminal with Mr Fazala and Miss S A Marcos.
2000 hours		Dinner with Miss Marcos, Mr Jurey and Mr P Newcastle at the Comcoriel Hotel.

Thursday, 15 July

0845 hours	DEPART	Comcoriel Hotel by Company car.
0850 hours	ARRIVE	Norwich Branch Office.
0900 hours		Meeting with Branch Office staff.
1130 hours	DEPART	Norwich Branch Office Helipad.
1235 hours	ARRIVE	Head Office Helipad.

itinerary

J

job description A document giving full details of a job vacancy, including details of the activities to be performed by the person undertaking the job and the standards to be achieved in carrying out the work.

job specification A detailed explanation of the type of person required to fill a given post, including the educational qualifications, previous experience, skills and personal qualities required.

justification A term referring to the way in which text starts and finishes relative to the left and right margins of the document. A justified left margin is one in which all text starts at the left margin position. A justified right margin is one in which all text finishes at the same point, giving an even right margin, as compared with a ragged right margin. When text is justified at both the left and right margins it forms a neat block. In word processing this is achieved by the automatic insertion of additional blank (soft) spaces between (or within) words. (See **ragged right margin**.)

justification function The justification function is used to change the left and right margins from ragged to justified and vice versa. Although it is possible to use ragged or justified margins at the left or right, in practice it is only the right margin that is changed from justified to ragged and vice versa. On most word processors it is possible, within one document, to have some sections with justified margins and some with a ragged right margin, if this is desired. The justification function usually operates like a toggle switch, with justification being shown on the format display as ON or OFF.

HEYDERFORD HYDRAULICS PLC

J O B   D E S C R I P T I O N

CLERICAL STAFF

JOB TITLE	Word Processor Operator
GRADE	Clerical 4
DEPARTMENT	Purchasing
LOCATION	Head Office
ACCOUNTABLE TO	Purchasing Manager
JOB SUMMARY	Providing word processing and general clerical support to the staff in the Purchasing Department, and undertaking responsibility for defined duties as outlined below.
PRINCIPAL DUTIES	1 Producing correspondence, agendas, minutes, reports, etc, required. 2 Preparing enquiries and orders as required. 3 Checking goods received notes against purchase orders and amending records as necessary. 4 Assisting with miscellaneous projects at the direction of the Purchasing Manager. 5 Maintaining and amending computerised purchasing control records, under the direction of the Purchasing Supervisor. 6 Filing general correspondence, agendas, minutes, catalogues, reports, etc. 7 Arranging service and maintenance calls by service engineers for the word processor and photocopier under the service agreement and maintaining a record of such calls.

JD/WPO/P/94

job description

K

keep function A word processing function which ensures that a vertical section of text is maintained as a block no matter where it is moved during the editing of a document. It is ideal for maintaining a table of figures as a block to ensure that it is not split between two pages.

kerning A term used in printing and desktop publishing programs in connection with the amount of space left between characters, and particularly between certain combinations of characters. The letters WA, for example, must be brought closer together than other characters to avoid the appearance of a wider gap between them than characters such as EM. The aim is to present visually consistent spacing between all characters.

keyboard An input device generally containing four rows of depressible blocks (keys) that are used to input information into an electronic device such as a computer or word processor, or, in the case of a typewriter, to cause characters to be printed on paper. The keyboard contains all the letters of the alphabet, the numbers 0 to 9, a variety of punctuation marks, accents and symbols, and a number of function or operational keys. The keyboard arrangement most commonly used in typewriting and word processing is known as the QWERTY keyboard because of the order in which the first six letters of the second row of keys is arranged. Other keyboard arrangements are available, including the Dvorak, Maltron and alphabetical keyboard arrangements.

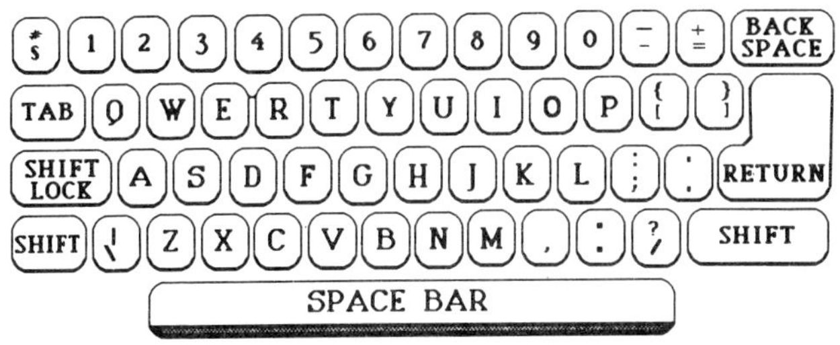

a QWERTY keyboard

keypad A small keyboard containing numbers and mathematical symbols, similar in appearance to the keyboard on a calculator. This may form an additional section on a QWERTY keyboard that is used for entering large amounts of numeric data. Keypads are also used for applications such as the control units for videotex terminals.

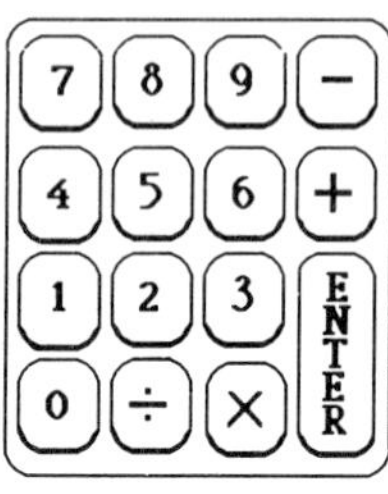

a keypad

key sequence The order in which a number of keys are pressed to carry out a particular word processing function.

keystroke The depression of a single key on the keyboard to enter a character or a hard space, or to input a command.

keystroke memory A word processing function whereby commands involving long and complicated key sequences for carrying out certain tasks can be saved and allocated to a single key or two keys. On some word processing systems the keys defined by the keystroke memory as the command keys are known as user defined keys.

keyword indexing The automatic preparation by a word processing system of an index or table of contents for a book or report from specific words that are indicated by a special coding system. When the command is given to prepare the index, the word processing system automatically selects all the coded words in a document and sorts them into alphabetical order in another document in the form of an index or table of contents.

kilobyte A byte is a single unit of memory in computing/word processing terms. One typing character is roughly equivalent to one byte. There are 1024 bytes in a kilobyte, although many people take a kilobyte as referring to a thousand bytes. The abbreviation K or Kb is used to represent the word kilobyte. Computer memory and disk storage capacity are usually given in terms of kilobytes available, eg, a 512 K or a 256 K computer.

L

landscape printing Using A4 paper with the longer side as the leading edge so that a wide document may be printed. (See **portrait printing**.)

lap-top computer (See **portable computer**.)

laser optical disk A non-magnetic storage medium with very high storage capacity. Information is written to the disk by a low power laser beam that etches the data on the surface of the disk in a series of pits. The data is scanned and read by a laser beam. The reading process does not involve physical contact, so there is no wear on the disk, as there is with magnetic disks. The stored data can be in the form of diagrams, plans, maps or photographs, handwritten, typed or printed text.

The acronym WORM, Write Once Read Many (times), is used to describe these disks because once data has been stored it cannot be erased or over-written. These disks are therefore used mainly in applications where vast quantities of information must be stored, but where amendment of the documents is not necessary or is undesirable, such as historical records or insurance policies. However, with the advance of technology, laser optical disks are being developed that will allow data to be written more than once.

laser printer A non-impact type of printer that produces very high quality printed documents containing text and graphics (diagrams or photographs) using photocopier technology. A whole page of text/graphics is output at a time, and for this reason laser printers are sometimes referred to as page printers. Laser printers are widely used with desktop publishing systems. (See **printer**.)

layout The format or display of a document. In desktop publishing terms this includes the arrangement of both text and graphics on a page.

leader dots Also known as leader lines. A series of dots, typed with the full stop key, that connect details at one end of a line of text to details at the other end, eg:

```
Standard Rose ...  ...  ...  ...  ...  ... £10.45
Climbing Rose ...  ...  ...  ...  ...  ... £15.25
```

Leader lines may be typed as a continuous row, or in groups of five, eg two dots and three spaces, three dots and two spaces or one dot and four spaces.

letter quality print (LQ) A print quality produced by a dot matrix printer that is considered equal to that produced by a daisywheel printer, ie, of a quality suitable for business correspondence.

Dot matrix printers are capable of printing in different qualities, including draft quality, near letter quality (NLQ) and letter quality (LQ).

letters Correspondence conforming to an accepted format. Business letters are generally typed on pre-printed paper headed with the company's details, though with the increasing use of microcomputers many small firms type these details at the top of the letter.

Business letters generally include the following parts: (*a*) a reference, showing the initials of the author and the typist, and possibly a file number; (*b*) the date on which the letter was typed; (*c*) the name and address of the recipient (the addressee or inside address); (*d*) the salutation, eg, 'Dear Sir' or 'Dear Mrs Scanlon'; (*e*) a subject heading identifying the content of the letter; (*f*) the main body of the letter; (*g*) a complimentary close, such as 'Yours faithfully' or 'Yours sincerely'; (*h*) the name of the firm from which the letter is sent; (*i*) the name and designation of the author; (*j*) the author's signature; and (*k*) the abbreviation 'Enc' or 'Att' to indicate that there is an enclosure.

The reference details and recipient's address are not generally included on personal letters.

light pen An input device for computers, shaped like a pen, on the end of which is a small light. The light pen is attached to the VDU by a cable. Data is input to graphics programs by placing the tip of the pen against the screen.

Another form of the light pen is used in retail shops and libraries for reading a bar code (a series of black lines of varying thickness representing numbers) printed on goods or books. When goods are purchased the light pen transmits the price and type of goods to the computer which gives a detailed printout on the bill and amends the stock records.

line drawing graphics function Some word processors offer the facility to draw horizontal and vertical lines, eg, around tables, organisation charts or flow charts. A printer must be used that can print out the lines.

line ending The end of a line of text indicated on the screen display by a symbol to show that the operator has keyed in a hard return with the return key.

Pre-printed letter heading	BESBRAND FOODS (UK) LIMITED UNIT 19 CAMPBELLE INDUSTRIAL ESTATE GIRTLETOWN GLASGOW G9 3RE TEL 041-333 773345
Reference	Our ref GC/DB/7701A
Date	12 May 199-
Addressee details	Mrs B Whiteside 132 Chinnery Farm Lane Springside Bridgenorth W16 4BT
Salutation	Dear Mrs Whiteside
Subject heading	BESBRAND BLACK CHERRIES
Body of letter	Thank you for drawing our attention to the faulty tin of Besbrand Black Cherries. We were sorry to learn that you had cause to complain about one of our products. The fault appears to be the result of an error by one of our high-speed automatic filling machines. We have now brought this matter to the attention of the Factory Manager concerned so that appropriate action may be taken to prevent a recurrence. We appreciate the opportunity you have given us to offer an explanation for the disappointment you felt, and enclose a refund to cover the cost of your purchase and the postal charges incurred in sending the package to us. We hope that you will continue to purchase our products and are confident that you will have no cause for further complaint.
Complimentary close	Yours sincerely
Company name	BESBRAND FOODS (UK) LIMITED
Signature	
Name	P R GOODWRIGHT
Designation	Customer Services Manager
Enclosure notation	Enc

a business letter

line numbering A function used when a draft document is to be revised. The word processor is given a command to number each line in the document. Numbering can be continuous throughout the document or can start afresh on each page.

line printer A type of printer used with large computer installations that prints at very high speeds. One line at a time is dealt with, all the As being printed first, then all the Bs, all the Cs and so on until the line of text is complete. (See **printer**.)

line spacing The distance between lines of text, usually expressed in terms of the number of lines of type to one inch. Line spacing may be set at single, one-and-a-half, double, or treble, ie 1, 1.5, 2 and 3. With single line spacing there are six line spaces to one vertical inch.

On a word processor the default setting is for single line spacing and this must be changed by the operator if alternative line spacing is required. Many word processors show the text in single line spacing on the screen whatever line spacing is selected, the actual spacing being adjusted when the document is printed.

Some word processing programs allow a wider variety of line spacing, particularly where a range of type sizes is available.

lines per minute (LPM) A measure of the printing speed of a line printer, which prints a line of text at a time, instead of a character at a time.

liquid crystal display (LCD) A flat screen display used in calculators and some portable computers consisting of two plates of glass with a special fluid between them. The liquid contains molecules that change to display characters on the screen when electrically activated. LCD screens are not as easy to read in strong daylight as other types of display.

list processing The manipulation of a list of data, eg, a record file of names and addresses. The records may be sorted into alphabetical, numerical or chronological order and specific records may be selected. The selected details, such as names and addresses, may then be merged with a standard document. (See **mail-merge** and **merge**.)

local area network (LAN) The linking together of various items of electronic equipment within a single building so that operators can communicate with other workers, to access shared databases and to share peripherals such as hard disk storage and printers. The LAN consists of a cable network, and may be a star, ring or bus network. (See **wide area network**.) (See page 77.)

log off A procedure involving commands to the computer or word processing system in order to terminate a session. Also known as log out.

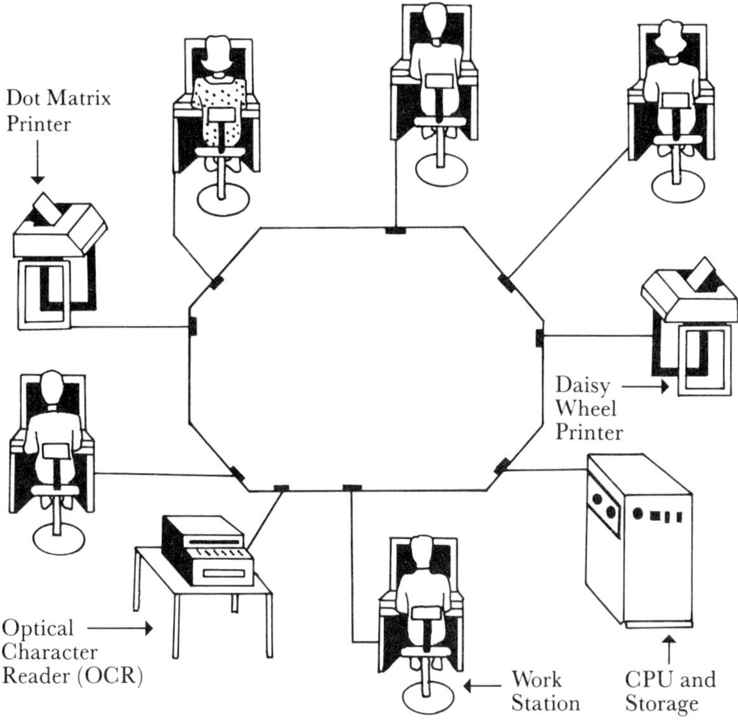

a local area network

log on A procedure involving commands to the computer or word processing system in order to start up the program, or to gain access to a shared/networked system. The operator may have to key in a password and an identification number before the system will respond and allow access to the program and the data stored on disk.

lower-case characters Alphabet characters that are not capitals. (See **capitals**.)

M

mail merge The automatic insertion by a word processing system of selected variable details stored in a data file into another document that contains coded insertion points to indicate the positions of the variable details. This produces a third document, known as the output document, containing all the necessary information.

The variable details generally consist of items such as names and addresses, and these may be merged with a standard letter to produce a series of personalised letters addressed to individuals. When the merge function is used to produce personalised correspondence and mailing labels, it is known as 'mail merge'.

If the printer is fitted with an automatic sheet feeder (hopper feed) or with continuous stationery, personalised letters can be merged and printed automatically at high speeds once the operator has given the merge command.

mailbox An electronic storage place for documents that have been transmitted by means of an electronic mailing system. The authorised user(s) can access the information stored in the mailbox by keying in a unique identifying code on a word processor or computer.

mailing list A list of names and addresses to which correspondence may be sent. The names and addresses may be in typewritten form, or stored on disk for use with a word processor. If the list is stored on disk in a special data file, it is possible to use the mail merge function to print the whole list or to print selected addresses from the list.

mainframe computer A very large, powerful computer system with many hard disks containing programs and data, that can be accessed by numerous terminals situated in different locations.

margin release A key that allows characters to be typed beyond the margin stop positions. The margin release may be used at the left margin to type an enclosure notation symbol within the left margin space. It may be used at the right margin position to allow the typist to complete a word that is too long to fit on the preset line length.

margins The white space surrounding a document. To give a good appearance to a typewritten or word processed document you should leave a minimum of one inch for each margin wherever possible. It may, in some cases, be necessary to reduce this minimum, and in some public examinations the minimum width is expressed as an aggregate (average) of one inch, but narrow margins of this size should be avoided wherever possible.

Margin stops are used on a typewriter to set the left and right margins, but the typist must ensure that the appropriate number of line spaces are allowed for the top and bottom margins. It may be found helpful to use a backing sheet on which are ruled black lines to represent the top and bottom margin positions.

On a word processor the left and right margin positions are determined by the default setting, or are set by the operator on the ruler line. These margin settings determine the length of the typing line. The default top and bottom margin settings may be overridden by the operator, if required, to alter the page length of a document.

The top and bottom margin spaces are sometimes referred to as the header and footer areas. (See **header** and **footer**.)

A justified margin is one in which every line ends at the same position so that the text forms a neat block. This is achieved by the automatic insertion of additional blank (soft) spaces between words. A ragged right margin is one in which each line of text starts at the left margin but ends at a different point, depending on the number of words that can be fitted along the line length. A ragged left margin is one in which each line of text starts at a different point and ends at the same point (ie as a justified right margin).

margin stops The mechanical devices used on a typewriter for setting the left and right margins.

marking a block A word processing operation involving the identification of a section of text on which a specified function will be carried out. A special mark or symbol is keyed in at the start and end of the text to be identified, this section then being referred to as a 'block'. The block may be highlighted in some way, eg, by reverse video. The operator then keys in the command sequence necessary to instruct the system to embolden, underline, delete, cut, move, etc, the whole block of text.

master file A master document, or template, containing a specific format for a document that is frequently used, such as a memo, letter or agenda. The master file may also contain some text that is always required, such as the letter heading, or the standard agenda details. When, for example, a letter is to be typed, the master file may be copied. The letter is typed on the copied file, leaving the original untouched so that it can be copied again when required.

mathematical signs and symbols Most keyboards contain at least a few mathematical signs and symbols, usually those most frequently used in general work, ie:

-	minus	'	feet
+	plus	"	inches
=	equals	%	per cent
x or *	multiplication	.	decimal point
÷ or /	division	@	at

Many electronic keyboards contain a wider range of symbols that may be used when typing mathematical data.

megabyte (M, Mb or MB) A unit of measurement of computer memory or disk storage capacity representing 1024 000 bytes (the M representing a million). A byte is a single unit of memory and one typing character is roughly equivalent to one byte. Many people use the term megabyte loosely to refer to 1 000 000 bytes.

memorandum (memo) An item of correspondence for distribution within a company, ie, for internal circulation. Memos may be typed on pre-printed paper that includes the printed headings MEMORANDUM, FROM, TO, REFERENCE and DATE. There may also be a special space with the title SUBJECT. Text should be carefully aligned against these header items. Alternatively, memos may be typed on plain paper, in which case the header items should be typed at the top of the page, together with the information relating to them.

A memo differs from a business letter in that it does not include a full address, the name of the recipient and department or branch usually being sufficient. The salutation and complimentary close are also omitted. Memos may be signed by the writer in full, or with the sender's initials only. In some organisations it is the practice to send memos without any signature.

Memos are sometimes distributed without being inserted into envelopes, but where an envelope is used it is generally only necessary to type the name and department (or branch) on the front of the envelope.

When memos are typed regularly on a word processor, it is a good idea to set up a master document (or template) with the format set for the appropriate line spacing, margins, etc, and the header items already keyed in. When a memo is to be typed the master document can be copied for use in producing the memo, leaving the original untouched ready for further use. (See page 81.)

memory A computer device or storage medium that can store and retain information for later retrieval. The term 'memory' includes the computer's main store and backing store, and storage media such as disks or magnetic tape. The computer's memory is usually described in terms of megabytes or kilobytes. A microcomputer, for example, may be described as a 128K or 256K system.

	M E M O R A N D U M
Sender's details	FROM Mr B R G Cooke Travel Department Head Office
Recipient's details	TO Miss L W Player Research Department Regency Works
Sender's reference	REF BRGC/LPJ
Date	DATE 14 June 199-
Subject heading	TRIP TO VANCOUVER AND ALASKA 3 JULY TO 15 JULY 199-
Body of memo	I enclose a detailed itinerary for your trip to Vancouver and Alaska next month, together with the necessary tickets and vouchers. Your currency and traveller's cheques will be issued at the end of this month. Please let me know as soon as possible if you need any further information or help.
Sender's initials	[signature]

a memo on plain paper

menu A list of word processing functions displayed on the VDU screen that indicates the options available to the operator at any given stage in word processing operations, eg:

```
                    M A I N   M E N U

C  Create a new document          I  Index display
D  Duplicate a document           P  Print a document
E  Edit an existing document      Q  Quit the system
H  Help file                      S  Spelling check

     Key in the character for the desired function
                and press the RETURN key.
```

Procedures generally start from a main menu, which may then lead on to a series of sub-menus. You may, for example, select the print option by keying in the character P, or by moving the cursor on to the P and pressing the return or enter key. A print sub-menu will then be displayed on the screen, offering a further list of options.

Menus may take up the whole of the screen area, or they may be displayed in the top few lines of the screen. Some systems have what are known as 'pull-down menus', which are usually operated with the aid of a mouse input device. A single line of options is displayed at the top of the screen. When the selected option is highlighted by moving the cursor on to it and holding down the mouse button, a block is 'pulled down' on top of the screen text giving options from a sub-menu. If, for example, the style option is chosen the sub-menu may list bold, italic, underline and centring functions.

Menus make it easier for new operators to learn to use the system, ie they are 'user friendly', as compared with word processing programs on which functions are activated by typing in a series of keystrokes such as 'COMMAND, J, R, T, ENTER' (for justifying the right margin of text). The menu listings avoid the necessity for memorising keystroke sequences of this kind.

menu based system A word processing program that operates through a series of menus is known as a menu based, or menu driven, system.

merge The combining of details from two files of information in order to produce a third file, or document, automatically. Name and address details may be merged with a standard letter to produce a personalised letter for each of a number of customers whose details are stored in a data file. (See **mail merge**.)

message switching An electronic method of despatching information generated on a computer or word processor to similar equipment in a remote location, either in the same country or on the other side of the world. The message is automatically transmitted, via relays called switching offices or centres, and passed on, possibly by means of a satellite, for transmission to the addressee's electronic mailbox or terminal.

microchip An integrated circuit device built up on a wafer of silicon that is used in the construction of computers. Also known as a chip or silicon chip.

microcomputer (micro) A computer system small enough to fit on a desk top, generally consisting of a central processing unit, a disk drive, a visual display unit and a printer. They are also referred to as PCs (personal computers) or executive workstations. The memory size of these computers is increasing so that the distinction between very powerful microcomputers and minicomputers is becoming blurred. A microcomputer may be linked to other terminals and peripherals via a network, or used as a terminal to a mainframe computer.

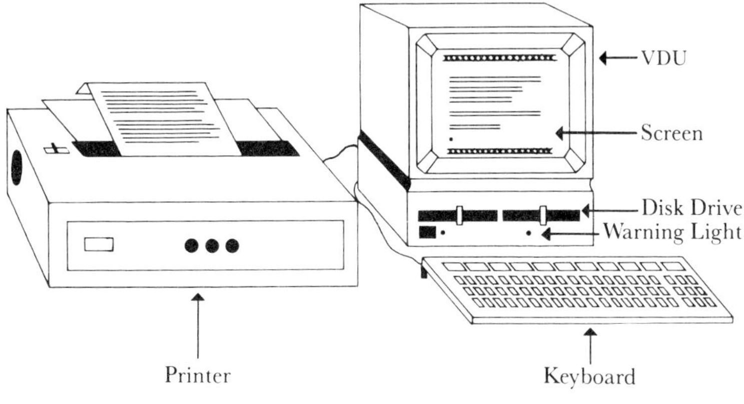

a microcomputer

minicomputer (mini) The name given to computers that are smaller, and less powerful, than mainframe computers. A minicomputer is capable of supporting a number of terminals, word processors, printers and other peripheral devices.

minutes An official record of the proceedings of a meeting, giving the names of those present and briefly recording each discussion point and its outcome. Each record may be identified with a number for easy reference. Minutes may be displayed in a variety of ways, depending on the needs of the organisation concerned, but marginal (side) headings provide a very clear and effective layout.

mode The method of operation of a word processor at any given time. Most systems may be used in either the insert mode or the overtype mode. When insert mode is in operation any text added to an existing document will be inserted at the cursor position, pushing forward the existing text, which is then automatically reformatted. When overtype mode is in operation any text that is added will by typed over the existing text, thus deleting it and any commands that are associated with it. Care must therefore be taken when keying in text in the overtype mode.

modem The abbreviated form of the words *MO*dulator-*DEM*odulator, describing a device that converts digital signals from a word processor or computer into analogue signals for transmission over the telephone network. A modem is required to transmit electronic messages from one computer or word processor to another at a remote location, and to convert the message back into digital signals that can be recognised by the computer system at the receiving end.

CARBERRIE WILDLIFE PARK AND ZOO

MINUTES OF THE FORTIETH PLANNING MEETING HELD AT 1430 HOURS ON FRIDAY, 14 SEPTEMBER 199-, IN THE AMAZON ROOM

PRESENT Mr Bernard Craike (Chair)
Mr Gordon Dresden (Secretary)
Miss Remi Frensham
Mrs Angela Hightown
Mr Ali Shariff

MINUTE NUMBER			ACTION
9/276	APOLOGIES FOR ABSENCE	Apologies for absence were received from Mr Raj Patel and Mrs Sandi Rainbird.	
9/277	MINUTES OF LAST MEETING	The minutes of the meeting held on Friday, 21 July 199-, were approved as a correct record and signed by the Chair.	
9/278	MATTERS ARISING	There were no matters arising from the minutes of the last meeting.	
9/279	FACILITIES AT PICNIC SITE	As a result of a number of complaints received about the distance of the picnic site from the nearest toilet block, it was agreed that additional toilet facilities should be provided in the woods close to the picnic area. Mr Dresden agreed to obtain prices and details of portable units before the next meeting.	GD
9/280	PROPOSED NEW ATTRACTIONS	Miss Frensham tabled proposals for an Adventure Trail and a Farmyard Corner. After lengthy discussion it was agreed that Miss Frensham and Mr Shariff should produce a report itemising the costs of setting up and operating these schemes.	RF and AS
9/281	ANY OTHER BUSINESS	There was no other business.	
9/282	DATE OF NEXT MEETING	The next meeting was arranged for Friday, 17 November 199-.	

minutes of a meeting

mouse A hand-held input device used to supplement the keyboard for moving the cursor, highlighting text and entering commands. The mouse, which is linked to the word processor by a cable, consists of a small box that fits neatly into the palm of the hand. On top of the box are one, two or three buttons, depending on the type of mouse used, and underneath the box is a rotating ball device.

When the mouse is rolled across a small area of the desk top, or a 'mouse mat', the cursor can be moved over the VDU screen. Depression of a button on the top of the mouse fixes the cursor on the screen and sets the typing point. By pressing or 'clicking' a button and dragging the cursor across the screen, text may be highlighted. Functions may then be carried out on the marked block of text by selecting the appropriate option from a pull-down menu, such as emboldening, centring or deleting the highlighted text.

The mouse is very easy to use and the movement of the cursor can be controlled very accurately. This device was introduced to appeal to people who were not accustomed to using keyboards, but it has now gained acceptance as a useful input device for all types of user.

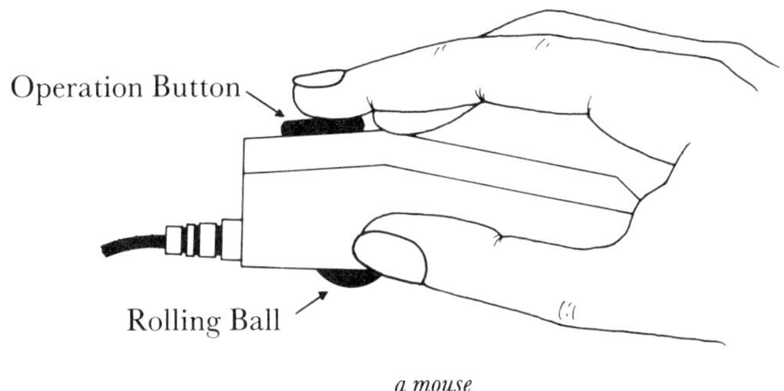

a mouse

mouse mat A small rectangle of specially treated anti-static material placed on a desk top so that a mouse device may be rolled across its surface. This prevents the mouse picking up dust, etc, from the top of the desk and controls the amount of space required for using the mouse.

move function The movement of a **'block'** of text from one position in a document and its insertion in another area of the document, generally by means of the cut and paste functions. The block of text to be moved is highlighted or marked with special coded symbols. (See **marking a block**.) It is then cut with the cut command. The cursor is moved to the position at which it is to be inserted and the paste command given. On a few word processing systems the text to be moved may be 'travelled' over the existing text until it reaches the position for re-insertion into the document.

Text may also be copied and the copy pasted into a new position, leaving the copied block of text in its original location, ie the section of text will then appear twice in the same document.

movement of text Text may be moved vertically in a document, as when a paragraph of text is cut from one position and moved up or down the page to a new position. Text may also be moved horizontally on some word processing systems, ie a column of text or figures may be cut from a table and moved across to the left or right of the screen so that it can be inserted at a new position in the table.

N

naming a disk The word processing program will not recognise a disk that has not been identified by a name. A name can be allocated electronically to a disk during the formatting or initialising procedure. Once the disk has been named you should write the name on a label and stick this on to the disk so that it can be identified in the disk storage box when required for use in the word processor. The disk name should be related to the type of information that will be stored on it, eg, REPORTS, MEMOS or MINUTES. On some systems the disk name may be restricted to about eight characters, and it may not be possible to use certain punctuation marks or symbols in the name. A disk may, if necessary, be renamed by using a renaming function.

naming a document (or file) Each document, or file, stored on a disk must be given a name to identify it, so that it can be listed on the directory or index of the disk. On some systems the document name may be restricted to about eight characters, and this can cause problems with choosing suitable names that describe the content of the document. In addition, such systems may not accept characters such as / , & : or . in a document name.

Wherever space allows, you should allocate a filename that describes the content of the document clearly, so that you can easily identify a document you are searching for even if it is some months since you last used it. If necessary, documents can be renamed through a rename function.

NCR An abbreviation for No Carbon Required, which refers to a special type of paper for producing multiple copies. NCR paper eliminates the need to insert carbon paper between sheet(s) of paper. It is specially treated on the reverse side so that anything typed on the top copy will automatically be reproduced on the sheets below. NCR sets may consist of several sheets, sometimes of different colours, attached together in such a way that they can be easily separated after typing. An invoice set, for example, will enable the invoice, copy invoice, delivery note, copy delivery note, etc, to be produced at the same time, either in a single set in the typewriter or in the form of continuous stationery for use in a computer or word processor printer.

near letter quality (NLQ) A term describing the quality of print produced from a dot matrix printer that is considered to be almost as good as letter quality, ie suitable for business correspondence.

network A cable system that connects word processor or computer terminals and allows them to share resources such as the memory, printers, or optical character readers. In addition, terminals linked by a network are able to communicate with each other. (See **local area network**.)

no carbon required (See **NCR**.)

node A connection point in a communication network for the purpose of monitoring and/or switching communications.

notice of meeting A document sent by the meeting secretary to members of a committee or an organisation to inform them of the day, date, time and place of a forthcoming meeting. In practice the notice of meeting is often incorporated with the agenda, and within an organisation it may be produced in the form of a memorandum. For certain types of meeting it is necessary to comply with regulations specifying that at least seven days' or twenty-eight days' notice must be given, so that members can make arrangements to attend. Informal meetings within a company are often arranged at very short notice and the notice may be given verbally.

numbered and lettered paragraphs Paragraphs may be given an identification number or letter for ease of reference, especially in long documents. The most commonly used numbering or lettering systems are: arabic figures, 1, 2, 3, etc; roman numerals, i, ii, iii, iv, etc; alphabet characters, a, b, c, d, etc, or A, B, C, etc; and the decimal system, 1, 1.1, 1.2, 1.3, etc. Arabic, roman and alphabet paragraph identifiers may be typed with a bracket on each side, with a single bracket at the right or without brackets, eg, **(a), a)** or **a.** Brackets are not used with decimal numbers. Leave at least two clear spaces between the paragraph number/letter and the start of the paragraph.

numbers Arabic numbers may be expressed as cardinal numbers, which tell you how many items there are, eg, 1, 2, 3, or as ordinal numbers, which identify the order of items, eg, 1st, 2nd, 3rd. Depending on the context and the purpose of the document, both cardinal and ordinal numbers may be typed as words or figures. Although you should aim for consistent use of words or figures throughout a document, a certain amount of common sense is required to ensure that the text is easily read and understood. You should, for example, type '*We have one or two copies left*' not '*We have 1 or 2 copies left*' or '*There were 27453 customers*' not '*There were twenty-seven thousand four hundred and fifty-three customers*'.

COMPANY POLICY ON HEALTH AND SAFETY

1 All possible steps will be taken to ensure the health and safety of employees and visitors to Company premises and to prevent damage to Company property or employees' belongings.

2 It will be the duty of every employee in the Company to co-operate in every way possible in matters concerned with health and safety at work, so that the Company can fulfil its responsibility for health and safety at work.

3 It is the duty of all employees to conform to Company policy, to follow the safety codes of practice printed in this policy document and supplied to every employee, and to accept and carry out their responsibilities. In this policy the term 'safety' is defined as follows.

3.1 The prevention of any type of injury.

3.2 The promotion and maintenance of occupational health and hygiene.

3.3 The control of all situations potentially likely to cause damage to property and equipment.

3.4 The investigation and analysis of 'near-miss' situations.

3.5 Fire prevention and fire control.

4 All employees should contribute towards the maintenance of health and safety in the Company.

4.1 All employees designated as having specific responsibilities for Health and Safety must ensure that these responsibilities are adequately delegated in their absence.

4.2 Statutory regulations must be complied with at all times, but in addition all employees should contribute towards making the work areas as safe as possible.

4.3 All work methods must be appraised periodically to ensure that the safest possible methods are adopted.

decimal numbered paragraphs

numeric keypad An additional block of about twelve keys incorporated into the right-hand side of an electronic keyboard, or supplied as a separate unit and attached to the system by means of a cable. Keys for the numbers 0 to 9 are arranged in a similar manner to those on a calculator, and there is generally an additional enter key.

numeric keypad

O

off line A term used to indicate that a terminal or a printer is not connected to the main computer or to the network. If the printer does not respond when a document is sent to print, check the indicator lights to see whether it is off line. In such circumstances some word processors will display a message informing the operator that the printer is not responding and suggesting a check to see that it is switched on line.

on line A term used to indicate that a terminal or a printer is connected to the main computer or the network and ready for use. The printer may have an indicator light that comes on when the printer is on line and you should always check that this is illuminated before sending documents to print.

open a space function A word processing function that instructs the system to leave a specified number of line spaces clear of text, and to hold them together as a block of blank space. This function is used instead of inserting blank lines by pressing the return key, and it ensures that the block of space does not get split between two pages.

operating system A software program, such as CP/M or MS-DOS, that controls the computer system, the operation of applications programs (such as word processing) and the various input and output devices. When a word processing program is used on a microcomputer it is usually necessary, at the end of a session, to quit the word processing program and return to the operating system before the disks are removed and the equipment switched off.

operator A term referring to a person who is employed to use a computer or word processor.

optical character reader (OCR) An input device capable of recognising text produced with one of a range of special typefaces through a process of optical character recognition. The reader scans a document and translates the scanned print into a digital form that can be accepted by the word processor and displayed on the screen or stored on disk. The document may then be edited, if necessary, and printed or dealt with as any other word processing document.

The typewritten sheet is fed into the optical character reader in very much the same way as pages are fed into a photocopier. This input device saves time and eliminates the need to key in text already available in printed form, as long as it is printed in a font that can be recognised by the reader.

optical disk (See **laser optical disk**.)

organisation chart A diagrammatical representation of the structure of a company or other organisation, showing the different levels of authority and responsibility of various members of staff or departments, and the lines of communication between them. Organisation charts are usually presented in a vertical form, like a pyramid, but they are occasionally shown in a horizontal form, as if the pyramid were set on its side.

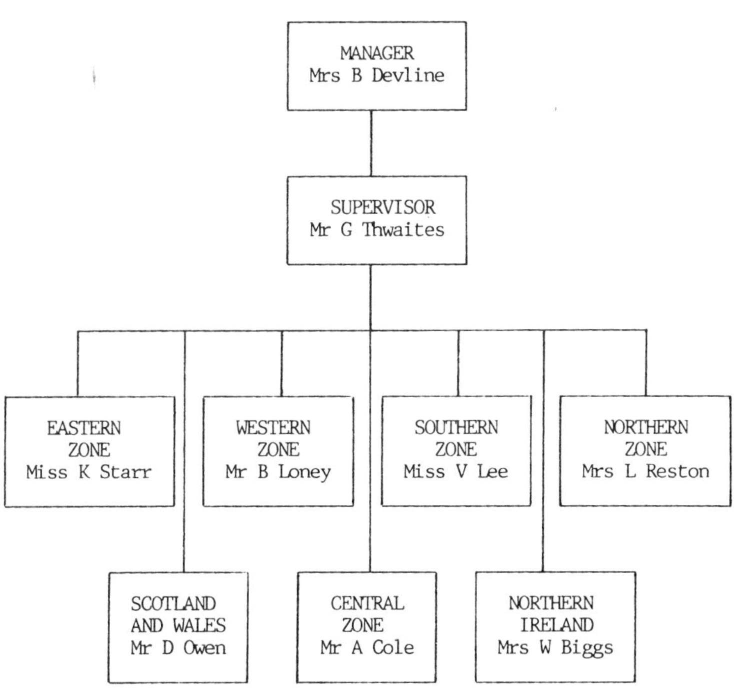

an organisation chart

originator The person who produces the first version of a document that will later be typed or keyed into the word processor whether it is by means of dictation, a handwritten or a rough draft keyed directly into the word processor. The word 'author' is more generally used to describe the originator of a document.

ornamentation (See **decoration**.)

orphan line The last line of a paragraph of text is called an orphan when it is separated from the rest of the paragraph by a page break. This is undesirable in layout terms, and the page length should be adjusted so that at least two lines are carried over to the next page. (See **widow line**.)

output Data that is passed from the word processor to another electronic device, eg, printed copy (hard copy) is the output of a word processor produced on a printer.

output device Output devices convert the information in the word processor into a form that can be read, and they include the screen of the visual display unit, printers and phototypesetters.

overstrike The facility offered on some word processors whereby a command can be given to allow one character to be typed over another so that the two characters occupy one unit of space. This permits the operator to produce a character or symbol that is not available on the keyboard. The combined characters may not be displayed on the screen in the form that they will be printed.

overtype The typing of one character over another on a typewriter. This is achieved by typing one character, pressing the backspace key once and typing the second character. Overtyping should be carried out only to produce combination characters that are not available on the keyboard, eg, S plus / will form $, c plus / will form ¢ and c plus , will form ç.

overtype mode (See **mode**.)

P

package A computer software program for use on a microcomputer, such as word processing, may be referred to as a package, or a software package. The package is usually accompanied by documentation in the form of a user manual, ie instructions on how to use the program. (See **applications program**.)

package–integrated (See **integrated software**.)

packet switching An electronic communications technique in which a complete message is automatically split up into one or more packets or segments for transmission through a network, and then reassembled into the original message at its destination. This compares with message switching where the whole message is transmitted. (See **message switching**.)

page In typewriting terms a page is a single sheet of paper on which text may be typed.

In word processing terms a page is the area available for text after the system has discounted the space allocated for the left, right, top and bottom margins (including any headers and footers). The default setting may be in the region of 80 characters wide by 58 lines long for an A4 page of text. Most word processors automatically move on to a new page as soon as a page is full. A marker may be displayed on the screen to indicate the end of a page and the start of a new one, eg, in the form of a dotted line or the characters NP (for New Page).

page break The point in a document where one page ends and another one begins, indicated on the screen by a line of hyphens, dots, or characters such as NP (for New Page). An automatic page break inserted by the word processor is known as a soft page break, or a dynamic or conditional page break. If the amount of text on a page is changed during an editing session, when words or paragraphs are added or deleted, the text is automatically reformatted to fit the page length.

A hard or forced page break is one inserted by the operator. It overrides the automatic page length allocated by the system, and can only be inserted at a point in advance of the soft page break. A hard page break remains in the same position in the text, even when amendments or deletions are made, until the operator keys in a command to delete the page break.

Page breaks are linked to a print control command that automatically ejects the page from the printer and feeds in another sheet from the paper cassette of a sheet feeder, or advances the paper to the correct 'top of page' position if continuous stationery is used.

page display The amount of text that is displayed on a VDU screen differs depending on the system used. Most word processors display as much text as will fit on half an A4 page, ie 80 characters by 25 or 26 lines. Some systems have a screen large enough to allow a full A4 page display, 80 characters by 50-60 lines.

page down A word processor function that removes the current display of text from the screen and replaces it with a display of the previous section of text in a document.In effect it moves the document down by one screenful of text. The cursor is automatically moved to the top left of the screen when this is done.

page layout The way in which text is displayed, or laid out, on a page, including line spacing, margin sizes, justification, centring, type size and paragraph style.

page numbering A document consisting of two or more pages should include page numbers on the second and any following sheets. The first page is not usually numbered. The page number may be typed in the top or bottom margin space, at the left margin, centred or at the right margin.

When a word processor is used the page numbers may be inserted in the header or footer space by means of an automatic page numbering function. A special code symbol is keyed in, such as CODE # , and the system will then automatically insert the correct page number on each sheet. If the number of pages changes after heavy editing, the system will automatically change the page numbers when the document is printed. The page number can be printed on every page, or on selected pages, eg, the operator may instruct the system to print page numbers from page 2 onwards.

The automatic page numbering function inserts the page numbers when the document is printed, but even if this function is not used each page of the screen document is numbered. This is useful when editing or moving from page to page of the document because the system can be instructed, for example, to 'Go to page 14', thus saving time scrolling through the document.

page printer A non-impact type of printer that prints a complete page of output at a time, very much in the way a photocopier reproduces a page of text. The whole page is usually stored within a buffer in the printer before printing starts. A laser printer is sometimes referred to as a page printer. (See **printer**.)

page offset An instruction to the printer to start printing a specified number of spaces from the position set for the left margin.

page up A word processor function that removes the current display of text from the screen and replaces it with a display of the next section of text in a document. In effect it moves the document up by one screenful of text. The cursor is automatically moved to the top left of the screen when this is done.

paging The process of automatically inserting page numbers on a document consisting of several pages when using a word processor. (See **page numbering**.)

pagination The automatic division of a document into page lengths by a word processing system.

paper alignment Paper must be placed in a typewriter so that the top edge is in a straight line. If the paper is not straight when it has been inserted, use the paper release lever to take the pressure off the paper and adjust its position. Correct alignment may be checked against the alignment scale, just above the printing point, or by rolling the paper through the platen until the top and bottom edges can be brought together.

If single sheets of A4 paper are used in a word processor printer the alignment of the paper should be checked in a similar way.

paper bail A movable bar on a typewriter or printer fitted with small rollers to hold the paper firmly against the platen. The rollers should be positioned at the left, centre and right-hand side of the page.

paper feed A mechanism for moving paper behind and around the platen of a typewriter or printer. When a word processing printer is used the paper is automatically fed through the machine, as long as a constant supply of stationery is available. Cut sheets (eg, A4 sheets) may be stacked in the paper cassette of a hopper or sheet feeder ready for feeding into the printer. As each page is printed and ejected it is automatically stacked in a receiving cassette.

Continuous stationery is fed through the printer by means of a tractor feed mechanism fitted with sprockets spaced around two wheels positioned at each side of the printer. The sprockets engage the holes punched into the side strips of the continuous stationery to ensure an even, straight feed.

paper guide A small moveable plate situated on the paper rest of a typewriter and some printers, which is used to set the left-hand position of the paper in relation to the markings on a graduated paper scale. The paper guide should be positioned so that the extreme left edge of the paper is inserted into the typewriter at 0° on the scale. This ensures that other settings such as margins, tabulator stops and any centred items are correct in relation to the scale.

paperless office The ideal of the office of the future, or the electronic office, in which there would be no need for printed copies of correspondence and other documents. In the paperless office – if it ever comes into being – all documents will be filed electronically, all internal and external correspondence will be transmitted electronically and read as soft copy, and all business records will be kept on computer disk.

paper quality A general guide to the quality of paper used for business documents is given by the expression of its weight in grammes per square metre (gsm or g/m^2). This value is usually printed on the end of the packet by the paper manufacturer. Paper with a high gsm number, eg, 90 gsm, is thicker than that with a low gsm number, eg, 70 gsm. Bond paper of 80 or 90 gsm is used for the majority of business documents. Paper with a gsm of around 40 to 45 is known as bank paper or flimsy paper, and this is mainly used for making carbon copies.

paper quantities Paper is supplied for general business use packed in quantities of 500 sheets. A packet of 500 sheets is known as a ream.

paper rest A plate situated behind the platen on a typewriter which is used to support the paper as it moves around the platen. The paper rest is sometimes referred to as the paper table.

paper sizes There are three series of paper sizes: A, B, and C. The sizes most generally used for typewriting are A4, A5 and A6. The sizes, in millimetres, of the paper in each of the series are given below:

A0	841 × 1189	B0	1000 × 1414	C0	917 × 1297
A1	594 × 841	B1	707 × 1000	C1	648 × 917
A2	420 × 594	B2	500 × 707	C2	458 × 648
A3	297 × 420	B3	353 × 500	C3	324 × 458
A4	210 × 297	B4	250 × 353	C4	229 × 324
A5	148 × 210	B5	176 × 250	C5	162 × 229
A6	105 × 148			C6	114 × 162
A7	74 × 105			C7	81 × 114
				C8	57 × 81

Continuous listing paper used in tractor feed printers is available in a wide variety of sizes, including A4 (the size quoted including the perforated strips at each side). Very wide listing paper is available for wide printers.

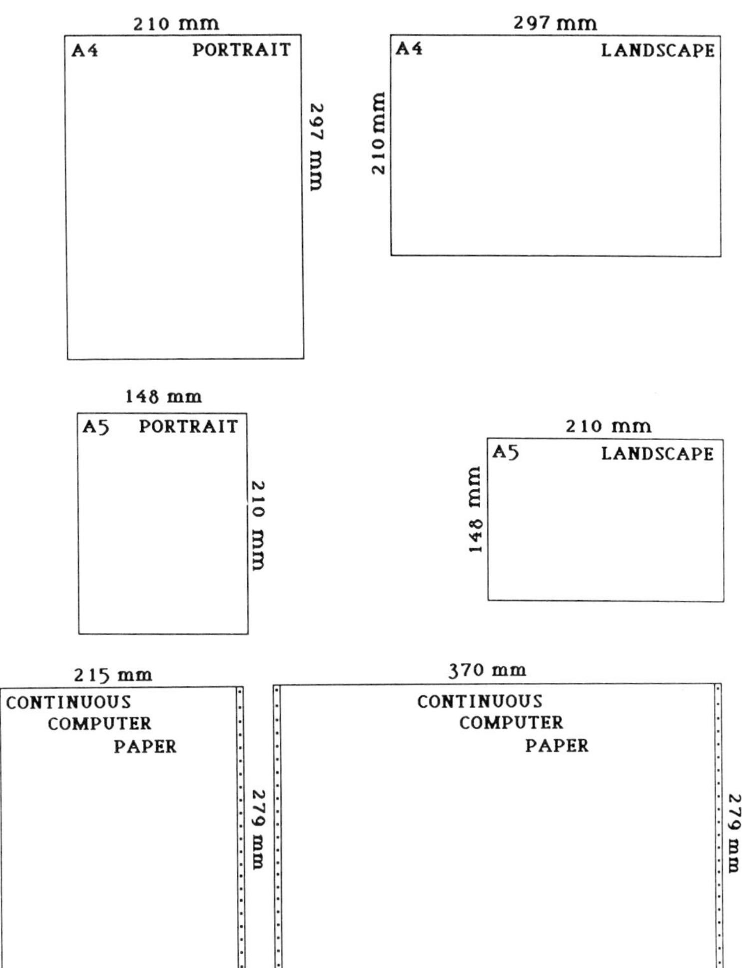

the major paper sizes

paper types Paper supplied in reams of 500 is known as single sheet or cut sheet paper. Continuous listing paper (also known as fanfold) is a long length of paper folded at perforated page lengths, generally supplied in boxes of 1000 to 2000 continuous sheets. Perforated strips at each side of the paper are punched with holes that correspond to sprockets on a tractor feed mechanism. When the printed pages are fed out of the machine they fall into a tray and automatically stack back into the fanfold position.

Carbon sets consist of a number of sheets of paper, either NCR or plain paper interleaved with one-time carbon paper, made into a set. This eliminates the need for the typist to spend time making up the sets. When one-time carbon paper is used the carbon sheets are removed and thrown away after printing. Carbon sets are available in single set form for use on manual typewriters, and as continuous stationery for use on word processor or computer printers.

paragraph numbering function Some word processors will, in response to the correct command, automatically insert paragraph numbers. This is particularly useful when typing a draft in which the author may wish to change the positions of certain paragraphs when the document is edited. When a paragraph is moved or deleted the numbers of all the following paragraphs are automatically renumbered. (See **numbered and lettered paragraphs**.)

paragraph styles or layout The simplest, quickest and most widely used style of paragraph layout is the blocked paragraph in which every line of text starts at the left-hand margin, or at an indented margin position, eg:

```
This is a sample of text typed in the blocked
paragraph style.  Every line of the paragraph
starts at the left margin.
1  This sample illustrates numbered paragraphs
   typed in the blocked style.

2  The paragraph numbers are typed at the left
   margin and each line of the blocked paragraphs
   starts at an indented margin position.
```

The first line of an indented paragraph is inset from the left margin by at least five character spaces. This may be done by setting a tab stop five spaces from the left margin, or by using an indented tab on a word processor that automatically insets the first line of each paragraph eg:

```
     This is an example of an indented paragraph
in which the first line of each paragraph is
inset from the left margin.

     The first line should be inset by at least
five character spaces, and preferably not more
than eight spaces.
```

A hanging paragraph is one in which the second line and all subsequent lines in the paragraph start two or three character spaces in from the starting point of the first line. Some word processors have a temporary margin facility that allows paragraphs of this kind to be typed eg:

```
The second and all following lines of a hanging
   paragraph are indented from the start of the
   first line by two or three character spaces.

Hanging paragraphs are time-consuming to type
   and their use should be avoided wherever
   possible.
```

password A code word that allows the authorised user access to word processing or computer files in order to prevent unauthorised people from reading or altering the information stored on the files. Passwords are commonly used on mainframes and minicomputers, but the facility is also available on many microcomputers.

When you start to log on to the system a screen message will ask you to key in your password, a string of numbers, alphabet characters or a combination of numbers and letters. When you type the password it is not displayed on the screen. This is a security measure to ensure that no-one inadvertently sees the password. Most systems will allow a maximum of three chances to key in the password, but if the correct password is not entered at the third attempt the computer will not allow you to progress any further. On some large computer systems a message will automatically be passed to the Computer Manager that an unsuccessful attempt has been made so that a possibly unauthorised user can be identified.

You should never reveal your password to anyone else, and it is good practice to change the password frequently. Obvious password codes like your name, initials or birthdate should be avoided, but on the other hand you must select a password you can remember easily.

peripheral A computing term referring to any equipment that is connected to the computer by a cable in connection with input, output, storage or transmission of text, including the keyboard, the mouse, the disk drive(s) and the printer.

per pro (pp) Strictly speaking the abbreviation *pp* or *per pro* (short for *per procurationem*) against a signature indicates that the person signing a letter or other document is authorised to sign 'for and on behalf of' the organisation or individual sending the letter, eg:

```
Yours faithfully
pp MALVERT & KIRKDEAL ASSOCIATES

Jonathan P Wingate

Jonathan P Wingate
```

In practice many people incorrectly use the abbreviation when signing in place of the writer whether they have any legal authority or not. Some people regard the signing of a letter by someone other than the writer as a little discourteous. If it is necessary to do so, always sign your *own* name followed by the name of the writer of the letter, eg:

```
Yours faithfully
WITHERFIELD ESTATES LIMITED
Imogen K Larbury
  for
ALLAN WITHERFIELD
```

personal computer (PC) A desktop microcomputer originally aimed at the single user for personal computing activities, either in the home for the hobby enthusiast or as a workstation in a business organisation. (See **microcomputer**.)

photocopying A quick, clean and simple method of producing duplicate copies of documents, as a single copy or up to thousands of copies can be made from the same original. Photocopiers range from small desktop models that simply reproduce a document to the same size (1:1 ratio) to those which offer a large number of options, including zoom magnification, automatic exposure control, editing facilities, memories for frequently repeated jobs, automatic document feed and sorting attachments that automatically collate multi-page documents.

In addition to high volume copying, photocopying is used in many organisations to produce single file copies and limited run copies that would previously have been produced as carbon copies.

phototypesetter Specialist printing equipment for producing a page image on photosensitive paper ready for bulk printing. Phototypesetters may be linked to word processors, or may accept data stored on magnetic disks as a method of input.

phrase file Short items of frequently used text may be stored in a special phrase file, which consists of one or more save/memory areas. The phrases are identified by an alphabetic or numeric code, and recalled when required for automatic insertion into a document. This may be done simply by pressing one or two keys, eg, PASTE 3, which will paste in the phrase identified as number 3. Phrases such as 'Dear Sir', 'Yours faithfully' and the names of the company and various executives may be stored. This facility is particularly useful for saving time and ensuring accuracy where the phrases contain difficult or unusual spellings. (See **abbreviations file**.)

```
 (1) Our ref  DWS/RMWP
 (2) Dear Sir
 (3) Dear Madam
 (4) Thank you for your letter of
 (5) Cuddly Toys Range
 (6) Educational Toys Range
 (7) Developmental Toys Range
 (8) We look forward to hearing from you.
 (9) Yours faithfully
     BROTHER RABBIT TOYS AND GAMES LIMITED
(10) Dervla W Strickland
     Customer Services Manager
```

a phrase file

pica A size of type. In typewriting pica type measures ten character spaces to one inch. In printing and desktop publishing terms, a pica is a unit of measure equal to one-sixth of an inch, or 12 points.

pitch A measurement indicating the number of characters that can be typed in the space of one horizontal inch across the line. The pitch sizes most commonly used in typewriting and word processing are 10, 12 and 15, giving ten, twelve or fifteen characters to the inch. (See **pica** and **elite**.)

pixels A term derived from the words 'picture element'. Characters on the VDU screen of a word processor or computer are made up of many rectangular elements, ie the pixels, which contain data representing the brightness (and, where appropriate, the colour) of the image. The best screen picture is obtained on a screen with the highest number of pixels. A screen consisting of 1024 by 768 pixels is considered a high resolution screen.

platen The hard roller in a typewriter or printer around which the paper rotates and against which it rests when printing takes place.

plotter A computer output device for producing drawings, diagrams and text on paper in one or more colours. Different types of plotter are available, including the flat-bed plotter which consists of a base, a paper table, a number of pens and a movable arm. The moveable arm selects a pen and moves to print the part of the drawing appropriate to that colour in response to signals from the computer.

point A term referring to a unit of measure, used in printing and desktop publishing. The point is the smallest unit of typographic measurement. There are 12 points in a pica, and 72 points in an inch.

This is an example of 12 point type size.

This is an example of 14 point type size.

This is an example of 18 point size.

This is an example of 24 point size.

pointer A name given to the screen position indicator on a word processor when a mouse input device is used. The pointer may, for example, be in the form of an arrowhead. The mouse is moved until the pointer is in the appropriate position and when the mouse button is 'clicked' the cursor is inserted at that point. (See **mouse**.)

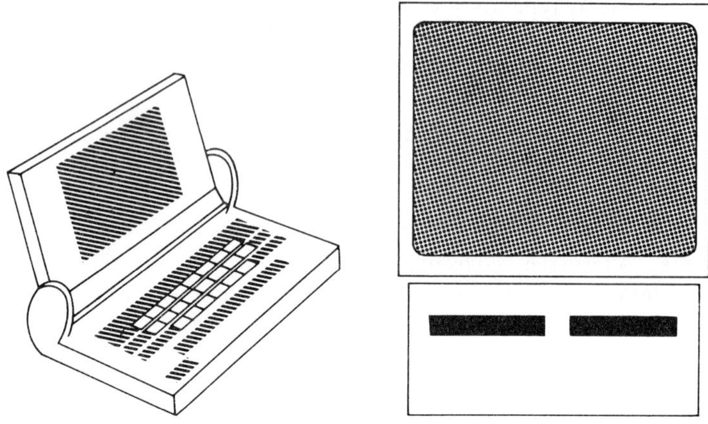

a portable computer compared in size with a personal computer

port A connection point at which an input or output device (eg, mouse or printer) may be connected to a word processor or computer or a data network.

portable computer A microcomputer small enough to be carried around for use by people whose work takes them away from the normal working base, also known as a lap-top computer. Portables generally incorporate a flat screen that can be raised when the equipment is in use, but which folds flat for transportation, making the unit into a convenient box or carrying case. Although they are intended for easy transportation, some machines are fairly heavy and have earned the name 'luggables' rather than portables.

portrait printing The normal printing orientation for an A4 page, with the shorter edge of the paper inserted into the typewriter or printer as the leading edge. (See **landscape printing**.)

postcard A postcard is used for business correspondence when the information it contains is not private. Cards are generally used for purposes such as change of address details, advice of the arrival of a maintenance engineer for an annual service or acknowledgement of the receipt of correspondence prior to it receiving attention.

The addressee details are typed on one side of the card. The sender's name and address details are typed (or printed) on the reverse side, along with the message. The message side may include the date, salutation and complimentary close details, but in many cases these are omitted because of restrictions on space. The date and recipient's address are often considered unnecessary on the message side because the address is typed on the front of the card, and the date is recorded in the form of the postmark. (See page 103.)

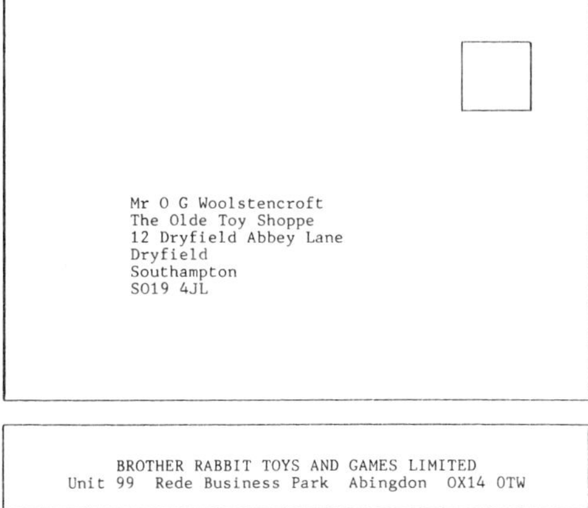

Mr O G Woolstencroft
The Olde Toy Shoppe
12 Dryfield Abbey Lane
Dryfield
Southampton
SO19 4JL

BROTHER RABBIT TOYS AND GAMES LIMITED
Unit 99 Rede Business Park Abingdon OX14 0TW

CHRISTMAS HOLIDAYS

Please note that our offices and warehouse will be closed from Thursday, 24 December, to Sunday, 3 January, inclusive. The latest date for receipt of orders to be despatched before the holidays is Friday, 18 December.

Thank you for your custom during the past year. We look forward to being of further service to you during the coming year.

Dervla W Strickland
Customer Services Manager

a postcard

postcript A supplementary note added to a letter, below the signature and any enclosure details, after the letter has been completed and/or signed. The letters PS should be typed at the left margin, followed by the postcript.

In desktop publishing terms, PostScript is a page description language used in connection with printing documents containing text and graphics.

posture The way you sit at the typewriter or word processor. Poor posture can lead to fatigue after sitting at the machine for even a short period. Ideally, your workstation should be so arranged that you can sit directly facing the typewriter or VDU screen, with your chair adjusted to a height that allows your feet to rest firmly on the floor or a footrest, with your thighs approximately parallel with the floor. The back of the chair should support your back in a slightly forwards position. The desk should be one designed specifically for typewriting or word processing. Small features such as the position of the copyholder, the ability to tilt and rotate the VDU screen to the correct position and correct lighting all affect the way in which you sit, and therefore your comfort.

prestel (See **viewdata**.)

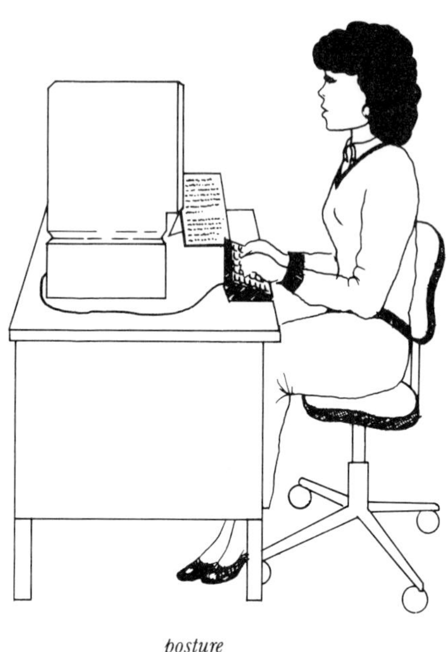

posture

preview A word processing function that allows the operator to display a document on the screen showing exactly how it will look when it is printed on paper, including centring, underlining, emboldening and line spacing. This is particularly helpful if the normal screen display on the system shows embedded commands for functions such as centring. Previewing is sometimes referred to as 'printing on screen'.

print control characters Some systems that are not able to display screen text exactly as it will be printed show characters on the screen that pass instructions to the printer for print enhancements, eg, ^C at each side of a section of text may pass a command for centring, ^E for emboldening or ^U for underlining. Although the print control characters appear on the screen they are not printed when a hard copy is made. It may also be possible to suppress the display of the print control characters on the screen so that the text may be read more easily when screen proofreading takes place. Print control characters may also be referred to as embedded commands or codes.

print enhancement Text may be emphasised in various ways to draw attention to the wording. This may be done by using bold print or underlining. In addition some systems, in conjunction with a dot matrix, ink jet or laser printer, are able to add emphasis to text by enhancing it as shown on page 105.

PRINT ENHANCEMENT

This is an example of plain text.

This is an example of bold or emboldened text.

This is an example of italic print.

This is an example of underlined plain text.

This is an example of outline print.

This is an example of shadow print.

print enhancement

printer The peripheral equipment required to produce a printed copy (hard copy) of a document from a word processor or computer.
Printers are divided into two main types: impact and non-impact. Impact printers use pressure against an inked ribbon to print the characters on the page. Dot matrix, daisywheel, thimble and line printers use impact technology.
Non-impact printers use neither pressure nor a ribbon for printing characters on the paper. Ink jet printers spray ink droplets directly on to the page; thermal printers use heat and specially treated paper to print the text and laser printers print whole pages, very much in the way pages are produced on photocopiers.

printing element (print head) The part of a printer that produces the characters and symbols available for a given typestyle. Daisywheel and thimble printing elements may be changed quickly and easily to provide an alternative typeface or type size. Dot matrix printing elements consist of a block of needles, the character or symbol required being printed by the selection of appropriate needles by the printer. It is therefore not necessary to change the print head when different typestyles are required.

printing from screen Printing operations carried out whilst the document is displayed on the screen. This may be done without saving the document. The screen document being printed cannot be edited, saved or manipulated in any way while printing is taking place.

printing in background (See **background printing**.)

printing on headed paper When pre-printed headed paper is used a deeper top margin must be used to ensure that the text begins below the printed heading. This may be done by changing the top margin space or by inserting additional blank lines with the return key before starting to key in the text. If single sheets are fed into the printer by hand, it may also be possible to turn the paper to the appropriate position in the printer ready for printing to avoid the need to change the top margin space.

printing point The point at which a character will be printed on the page. In typewriting the printing point may be referred to as the typing point.

print menu A list of options, related to the operations connected with printing a document on a word processor. The operator may select options or key in various choices, otherwise the default settings will be used by the system. The options available generally include selection of the document to be printed, the printer to be used, whether single sheet feed or continuous stationery is to be used, the number of copies required and the page on which printing is to start and/or stop.

P R I N T   M E N U

Print Options	Current Setting
Begin printing current file	APPTMTS
Select a file to print	----
Select printer to use	DMP4500
Number of copies to print	1
Begin at page	1
End after page	1
Continuous paper Y/N	N
Single sheets Y/N	Y
Send to print	PRESS RETURN

print menu

print pause A command that temporarily stops the printer during the printing process. This may be necessary so that you can attend to a problem such as changing the ribbon, adjusting the paper, removing damaged paper, and changing the print head, or even to silence the printer while you answer the telephone. Printing is suspended, but not cancelled, and the process can be started again by giving the 'print continue' command.

print queue A number of documents sent to the printer by one or more word processors linked through a local area network that are waiting their turn to be printed automatically as soon as the printer is free. A spooler (*S*imultaneous *P*eripheral *O*peration *O*n *L*ine) is required to store the documents until the printer is available. This frees the sending word processor and allows work to continue on another document. On some queuing systems documents can be given a priority code so that urgent documents are printed before routine documents.

print styles Print can differ in its shape (the font) and its size (points). The three main sizes available on typewriters are pica (10 characters to one inch), elite (12 characters to one inch) and micro (15 characters to one inch). Many word processing systems offer a much wider range of type sizes and styles. (See **font**.)

PRINT STYLES

This is an example of Chicago print style.	This is an example of Monaco print style.
This is an example of Courier print style.	This is an example of New York print style.
This is an example of Geneva print style.	This is an example of Times print style.
This is an example of Helvetica print style.	This is an example of Venice print style.

program A series of instructions given to a computer/word processor so that it can carry out specific procedures. (See **applications program**.)

program disk In word processing terms, the disk containing the word processing program, as compared with the working disk (or data disk) that contains stored text.

programmed key sequences Some word processors allow long and complicated key sequences to be keyed in, stored in memory and allocated to a single key, sometimes referred to as programmable keys or user defined keys.

prompts An instruction, question, reminder or statement displayed on the VDU screen to prompt the operator to take further action or to provide a 'second thoughts' stage when an irretrievable action is to be taken. When a document is to be deleted the system may, for example, display 'Are You Sure?' so that the operator can check that the document really should be deleted.

Programs using screen prompts are said to be 'user friendly' because they help the operator and reduce the need to memorise or look up instructions. The prompts may be displayed on a special prompt line and may include items such as: 'Please Press Return' and 'Press Y for Yes or N for No'.

```
SAVE FILE:  B/MINUTES  DO YOU WANT TO SAVE CHANGES?    Y/N
                       Press Y for Yes and N for No
```

screen prompts or operator prompts

proof A sample of page layout for correction and approval by the author.

proofreading Reading and checking a document to ensure that it is a true copy of the original and does not contain any spelling, grammatical, typographical or formatting errors.

The responsibility for proofreading rests with the typist or word processor operator. All work produced on a typewriter or word processor should be proofread and compared with the author's original for correctness and completeness to ensure that the work is accurate, that nothing unnecessary has been added and that nothing essential has been omitted.

If you use a word processor the proofreading process should be carried out in two stages. The screen document should be checked before it is printed. When the text has been printed the hard copy should be proofread. Take particular care with names, addresses, dates, figures, measurements and amounts of money. If there is any doubt about the accuracy of an item, check this with the author of the document.

proportional spacing The allocation of space to each character in relation to the size of that character. The letter 'I', for example, is allocated less space than the letter M, and the word INITIALS takes up less space than the word TOMORROW. A proportional spacing typeface produces a printed document that is similar in appearance to a document prepared on phototypesetting equipment, and it is thought by many people to be easier to read than a typeface in which every character occupies the same amount of space.

protected space (required, quoted or coded space) A command may be given to a word processing system to protect a space between two words or groups of figures to ensure that they are never split between two lines. If, for example, you typed the words 10 pm, you would protect the space between the *10* and the *pm* to ensure that they were always treated as a block, in other words as one 'word processing word'. This function is useful when typing a date or a person's name. Even if the words appear in the middle of the line when keyed in, it is possible that later editing changes may move them to the end of the line. It is therefore good practice to insert protected spaces between groups of words such as *Mr A M C McKeown* or *24 May 1995* when they are keyed in.

When text is typed without protected spaces the words may be split by the wraparound function as shown below.

```
The meeting of the Tyland Tourism Committee on 25
March will be held in the Featherstone Room at 10.30
am, with Mr A R C Wilberforce in the chair.  Miss C V
Benson will act as Secretary in the absence of Mr L J
Cornwallis.
```

When protected spaces are used the words are kept together on the same line. Note that the protected spaces may be identified on the screen by a symbol such as dot, as shown in the example below.

```
The meeting of the Tyland Tourism Committee on
25˙March will be held in the Featherstone Room at
10.30˙am, with Mr˙A˙R˙C˙Wilberforce in the chair.
Miss˙C˙V˙Benson will act as Secretary in the absence
of Mr˙L˙J˙Cornwallis.
```

protecting a document A security procedure available on some word processing systems for preventing unauthorised people from gaining access to documents. A command is given to the word processor, usually through a menu option, which limits access to the named document. There may be different levels of protection: *(a) write protection,* which allows a user to access the document, read it and possibly print a copy but does not allow the text to be altered in any way nor the document to be deleted; *(b) read protection,* which lists the document in the index but does not permit it to be accessed and read by unauthorised users; *(c) copy protection,* which allows the document to be accessed but not copied or altered in any way; *(d) unlisted protection,* which means that a document may be stored on the disk but not shown in the directory or index so that an unauthorised user is not aware of its existence.

punctuation style Two methods of punctuating text may be used in typewriting: full and open style. With both styles all grammatically essential punctuation is included.

Full punctuation style involves the use of full stops after item numbers, abbreviations and the initials of names and between the letters of acronyms (for example, 1., Enc., e.g., i.e.,Mr. J.G. Wilson, B.B.C. and W.H.O.).

With open punctuation style, which is more generally used, full stops are omitted after these items (for example, 1, Enc, eg, ie, Mr J G Wilson, BBC and WHO).

putaside area (See **buffer memory**.)

Q

queue (See **print queue**.)

quit (exit) A word processing term referring to the facility for leaving a document and returning to the main menu, or leaving the word processing system and returning to the operating system program.

quoted space (See **protected space**.)

qwerty keyboard The standard keyboard layout used for most typewriters and word processors, which derives its name from the sequence of characters found on the first six keys in the second row, ie Q, W, E, R, T and Y. The QWERTY keyboard consists of a row of figure and symbol keys, three rows of characters and symbol keys, a space bar and several special function keys arranged at the left- and right-hand sides.

R

radio button A small circular symbol displayed on the VDU screen of some computers and word processors that acts as an on/off switch, often in conjunction with mouse input. The button may be displayed as shaded in with black when it is switched on, and white when it is switched off.

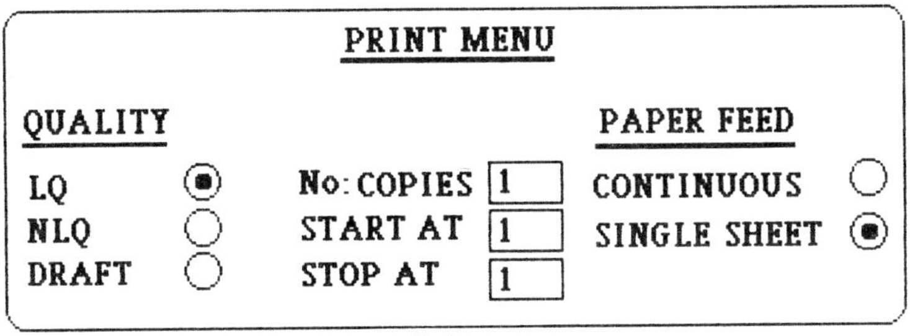

PRINT MENU

QUALITY				PAPER FEED	
LQ	◉	No: COPIES	1	CONTINUOUS	○
NLQ	○	START AT	1	SINGLE SHEET	◉
DRAFT	○	STOP AT	1		

radio buttons

ragged right margin A right-hand margin in which each line of text ends at a different point giving a ragged appearance, as compared with a justified right margin in which every line of text ends at the same scale point. (See **justification**.)

random access A method of rapidly accessing documents stored on a word processor or computer disk. The system can look for and retrieve data stored at any point on the disk. This compares with sequential access, eg for data stored on a tape, where the order in which the data was originally stored is the only order in which it can be read and accessed.

random access memory (RAM) A set of storage locations on a computer or word processor system. Any location can be written to and accessed directly at high speed.

read only memory (ROM) Computer or word processor memory that holds data permanently, which cannot be changed by the system or by the operator.

read/write head The device within a disk drive that reads data from a disk and writes data to a disk.

read/write memory A type of computer memory that can be written into as well as read, as compared with read only memory.

recalling a document to screen Bringing to the word processor screen a document that has been keyed in and saved to disk.

record A collection of details connected with a particular topic such as an individual, a company or a piece of equipment. A record contains a number of single items of information called fields, such as a person's name or address. Each field has a field name as shown in the example below.

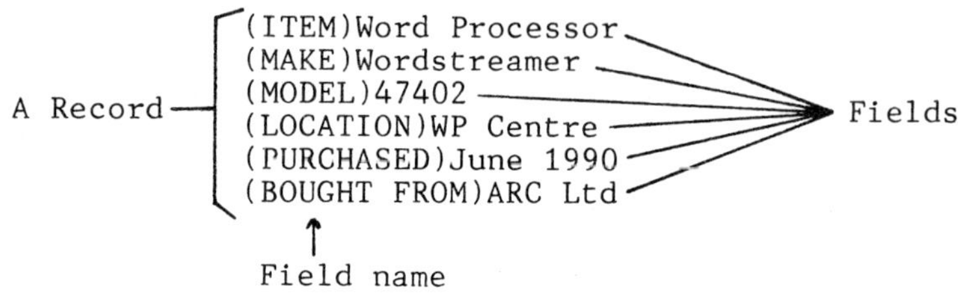

a record

record separators Records in a data file are separated from each other by means of record separators which may consist of symbols such as a pair of brackets.

records processing The manipulation and integration of data that has been stored on disk in a records data file. Information in the data file may be sorted into ascending or descending alphabetical or numerical order, or certain records may be selected and sorted. Selected information from the records may be inserted (merged) into word processing documents. The name and address of the recipient, for example, may be selected and automatically merged with a standard letter.

reference An identification code used on letters and other documents, generally indicating the originator (author) and typist of the work, eg, GMA/RSW or GMA/rsw. On correspondence it is usual to type the words 'Our Ref' followed by the reference. A reply to correspondence received may also quote the reference from the incoming letter as 'Your Ref'.

reference symbol A symbol placed within text referring to a footnote at the bottom of the page or at the end of the document, eg, the asterisk *, the dagger †, the double dagger ‡ and the section symbol §. (See **footnote**.)

reformatting The re-arrangement of text on a VDU screen after editing or alteration of margins, page length, typesize, etc. Reformatting is carried out automatically on most word processors, but on some systems it may be necessary to give a command to instruct the system to reformat the text a paragraph at a time.

reminder file (bring forward file or tickler file) A cardboard folder containing notes reminding you to follow up correspondence or any other document to ascertain that action has been taken as necessary, eg, the arrival of goods or an arrangement to hire audio-visual equipment for a meeting. It is usual to take an extra copy of any document that you wish to bring forward for attention so that it can be kept in the reminder file, which should be checked each morning for items requiring action that day.

rename function It may be necessary from time to time to change the name given to a document or to a disk. This may be done by selection of the rename function from a menu, or by following a series of operator prompts.

repagination The reformatting of edited text into appropriate page lengths on a word processing system.

repeat key A key that will repeat a character when it is held down firmly instead of being tapped once. On typewriters there is generally a limited number of keys that will automatically repeat characters in this way, but the majority of keys on an electronic keyboard operate as repeat keys. Repeat keys are useful if you wish to type a continuous line of full stops, underscores or characters for decorative purposes.

report An account of a process, development, or event such as a report on a vehicle assembly procedure, a research project or a publicity conference.

report format A word processing function where data, automatically taken from details contained in a records file, is merged with a word processing document and presented in tabular form. (See **record**.)

required hyphen (hard hyphen) A word processing term referring to a hyphen typed in by the operator from the keyboard. A required hyphen is a permanent or hard hyphen that will remain in the word, no matter where it appears on a line of text, unless it is deleted by the typist. (See **soft hyphen**.)

required page break (See **hard page break**.)

required space (See **protected space**.)

resolution The number of dots per inch used to represent a character on the word processor screen. High resolution screens provide a smoother image and have more dots to the inch than low resolution screens.

response time The time it takes for a word processor to react (respond) to instructions keyed in by the operator.

retention period The length of time specified by an organisation for which a document should be kept on disk before it is deleted, or the length of time for which paper documents should be kept in the files before they are destroyed.

return key A typewriter key that, when depressed, returns the carriage or the printing point to the left-hand side of the paper. The return key on a word processor keyboard is used to force a line ending, and it may also be used to enter a command to execute an instruction. On some electronic keyboards the return key may be labelled as the enter key. (See **hard return** and **soft return**.)

reverse video (inverse video) A method of highlighting to identify a block of text on which a word processing function or operation is to be carried out, by reversing the screen colours. If, for example, the normal screen displays black text on a white background, the reverse video display will show white text on a black background.

THE ORIGINAL SCREEN DISPLAY

SCREEN DISPLAY IN REVERSE VIDEO

reverse video

revision tracking (change bars) A word processing function whereby changes made to a document during the editing process are highlighted by a line placed through words that have been deleted and a line placed above words that have been inserted. Revision tracking can be helpful to an author for comparing editing changes with the original draft. An alternative is the use of change bars, ie vertical lines placed in the left margin to indicate a section of text in which editing changes have been made. (See **change bars**.) (See page 115.)

ribbon A narrow strip of inked material used on a typewriter or impact printer. When the print element strikes against the ribbon a deposit is printed on the paper in the shape of the character, figure or symbol required. Printing ribbons are available in two main types: fabric and carbon.

Fabric ribbons are available in various colours such as black, brown, blue or red, black being the most universally used. Typewriter ribbons are also available in two colours, the ribbon being divided horizontally into two halves, eg, the top half black and the lower half red (bi-chrome ribbons). Fabric ribbons are supplied on spools or in cartridges as a continuous loop, which is used repeatedly until the ink becomes too faint.

Carbon ribbons consist of a length of thin film coated with a carbon substance and are used only once because the carbon is deposited on the paper. They are available as single-strike or single-pass ribbons, which move along a whole character space at a time, or the more economic multi-strike ribbons which move along only a fraction of a character space at a time.

Special correction ribbons are also available for typewriters for correction of typing errors. (See **corrections**.)

Original typed version of paragraph

It is important for us to ensure that personnel records are always accurate and up-to-date. Please remember to ensure that the Personnel Manager is informed immediately of any changes to personal details such as name, address or telephone number. In addition, you should advise him of any extra educational qualifications you gain during your period of employment.

Handwritten amendments on the original passage

most our
It is important for us to ensure that personnel records are ~~always~~ accurate and up-to-date. Please ~~remember to~~ ensure that the Personnel Manager is informed immediately of any changes to personal details such as your name, address or telephone number. In addition, you should advise him of any ~~extra~~ new educational qualifications you gain during your period of employment with the company.

Edited text showing the revision tracking marks inserted by the word processor

It is most important for us to ensure that our personnel records are ~~always~~ accurate and up-to-date. Please ~~remember to~~ ensure that the Personnel Manager is informed immediately of any changes to personal details such as your name, address or telephone number. In addition, you should advise him of any ~~extra~~ new educational qualifications you gain during your period of employment with the company.

Edited text with revision tracking marks removed and amendments carried out

It is most important for us to ensure that our personnel records are accurate and up-to-date. Please ensure that the Personnel Manager is informed immediately of any changes to personal details such as your name, address or telephone number. In addition, you should advise him of any new educational qualifications you gain during your period of employment with the company.

revision tracking marks – a line is printed above newly-inserted text, and through deleted text.

roller An alternative name for the platen or cylinder of a typewriter or printer. (See **platen**.)

ruler cursor (dummy cursor) A line or other marker that moves along the ruler line on a word processor screen to indicate the horizontal column position of the true cursor on the line of text. On systems that do not have a ruler cursor the cursor position is shown by figures displayed on the status line, eg, L12, C57 indicates that the cursor is currently resting on line 12 at column number 57.

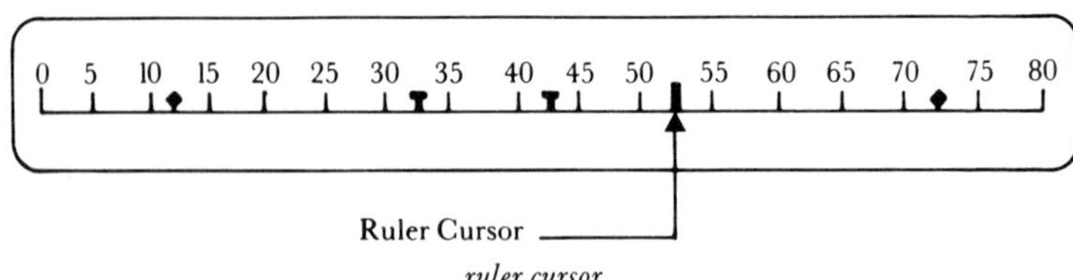

ruler cursor

ruler line (margin line, tab rack or control line) A line, or scale, displayed at either the top or bottom of the VDU screen to give information on the current positions of margins and tab stops, ie the ruler settings. The ruler line is divided into units representing the character spaces available, depending on the size of type being used.

The left and right margin positions are indicated by appropriate characters or symbols, eg, L for left, R for ragged right or J for justified right. Tab stop positions are indicated by a symbol such as ! for a normal tab and £ for a decimal tab stop, or by characters such as T for normal, D for decimal, C for centred and F for flush right tab stops, as shown in the example below.

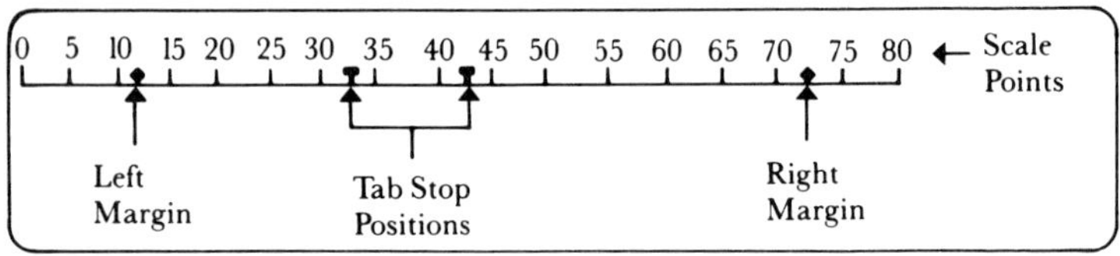

ruler line

On some systems the ruler line is combined with the status line. (See **status line**.)

rules (ruled lines) Continuous horizontal lines keyed in by means of the underscore, the underline function or a special line drawing function and used to separate items or areas of a page display. Some word processing systems also offer the facility for vertical lines to be 'ruled' on the screen and printed out.

running correction Correction of an error made by the operator when text is being keyed in.

running footer/header (See **footer** and **header**.)

S

salutation The courtesy opening to a letter, such as 'Dear Sir', 'Dear Dr Hill', 'Dear Mrs Jones' or 'Dear Sandra'.

save area (See **buffer memory**.)

save function The save function transfers documents from a word processor's memory to a storage medium such as a floppy disk. Some word processors save text automatically at regular intervals while text is being keyed in, whereas on other systems it is necessary to give the command to save. If you use a word processor of this type, make a habit of saving at regular intervals, eg, after typing half a screenful of text, so that if a system error or electrical fault occurs you will only lose the small amount of text that has not yet been saved.

A document must always be given a name before it can be saved so that it can be listed in the disk directory or index, and can be recalled to the screen by using that name.

scanner An input device for scanning and reading typed or printed text directly into the memory of a word processor, where it can be edited and printed in the same way as a document input from the keyboard.

scrambler A security device used in electronic communications for coding and transmitting messages in such a way that they cannot be read by unauthorised persons. When the message reaches its destination terminal it is unscrambled by a similar device so that it can be read and printed.

scratch pad memory A small memory used as a temporary storage space for data. (See **buffer memory**.)

screen The part of the visual display unit of a word processor on which text is displayed. It may be looked upon as a window which allows you to see what has been typed. Screens are available in a variety of colours, eg, white, grey, amber, green or brown, each with a contrasting colour of text display.

screen copy The output from a word processor as seen on the display screen. Also known as soft copy.

screen size The size of a VDU screen is generally stated in terms of the number of lines and columns of text that can be displayed on it, a column representing the amount of horizontal space occupied by one character. The majority of word processor screens are 80 columns by about 26 lines, ie the quantity of text that will occupy about half a page of A4 paper, known as a half page screen display. Some systems have a full page screen that displays 80 characters by 50 to 70 lines of text. Larger screens are available for special purposes such as desktop publishing layout.

scrolling The continuous movement of text from left to right, or from right to left, across the screen (horizontal scrolling), or up and down the screen (vertical scrolling), so that text not currently displayed on the screen area can be viewed.

Horizontal scrolling is used when a document wider than the screen area is displayed and vertical scrolling is used for documents longer than half a page of text. Scrolling can be carried out by means of dedicated scroll keys or by typing a command key sequence.

search (find) A word processing function that automatically looks through a screen document to find each occurrence of a given character, word or words, ie a 'string'. As each occurrence of the string is found it is highlighted in some way. The search function may be used for rapid movement through a long document when editing. You might, for example, command the system to search for a unique string such as *the new pension arrangements* and the text of page 7 containing these words would automatically be displayed on the screen. On a system that does not have the facility for moving the cursor sentence by sentence you can use the search function to move the cursor along a full sentence at a time, if necessary, by searching for the full stop followed by a character space.

On many word processors the search will only start from the cursor position onwards to the end of the document, so it is usual to ensure that the cursor is at the start of the document. Some systems do allow a backwards search to take place from the cursor position back to the beginning of the document. The search function may incorporate options for searching for a string exactly as keyed into the search option, or in any other form such as in capitals, underlined or emboldened.

The use of the search function without the replace option is sometimes referred to as search and display.

search and replace The search function is combined with a replace option that replaces each occurrence of the string found with an alternative string, eg, *car* may be replaced with *vehicle*. The search and replace procedure may be carried out automatically throughout the whole document on entry of the appropriate command, (this is known as a global search and replace). However, most operators prefer each occurrence of the string searched for to highlighted in turn so that a decision can be made about whether the word is to be replaced exactly, replaced with an alternative string or left as it is, as shown in the example below.

```
The needs of the company have been considered by our
consultants, Mather and Company, who have issued a
report entitled CHANGES IN THE STRUCTURE OF THE
COMPANY.  Mather and Company have also made a short
video film to accompany the report.  All members of
the company will see the report and film.
```

```
The needs of the organisation have been considered
by our consultants, Mather and Company, who have
issued a report entitled CHANGES IN THE STRUCTURE OF
THE ORGANISATION.  Mather and Company have also made
a short video film to accompany the report.  All
members of the organisation will see the report and
film.
```

search and replace

The word *company* has been replaced by *organisation* on the first and last occasions and by *ORGANISATION* in the name of the report, but *Company* has to be retained in the name of the consultants. In addition the string *company* occurs in the word *accompany*, but this must not be replaced with *organisation*.

security Any paper documents, microfilm or disks containing confidential or sensitive information should be kept in a safe and secure location. Many organisations allocate various levels of classification to documents, disks or other information, such as 'confidential' or 'secret'.

In addition, care should be taken to ensure that any discarded records, waste or scrap is thoroughly shredded or incinerated and that materials intended for destruction are kept in a secure place until they are destroyed. Items such as carbon-film ribbon cassettes should be incinerated if they have been used for typing classified information.

If you work in a department such as Personnel, where information of a personal nature concerned with staff records may be displayed on the screen of your word processor, you should make sure that the screen cannot be read by casual visitors to the office. Always lock away confidential papers and disks when you leave your desk.

THE DATA PROTECTION ACT places on an organisation the responsibility for ensuring that any information stored on a computer or word processor is made secure from external and internal access, except by authorised people.

Premises and equipment must also be made secure, and many

organisations operate staff badge identification systems and restricted entry procedures. All equipment should be listed on an inventory, showing the serial number of each machine, and wherever possible equipment should be marked with the name of the organisation. Valuable items and disks containing important information should be kept in a fire safe when not in use to protect them from possible damage by fire. (See **Data Protection Act, password, protecting a document, scrambler**.)

security copy (See **back-up disk**.)

security system The overall procedure adopted by an organisation to ensure that the grounds, buildings and their contents are kept secure from external and internal interference. The security system may involve control of access into the building and to specialist rooms within the building. (See **security**.)

selective printing A method of instructing a word processor to print specified pages from a long document instead of the whole document, eg:

pages to print	5 –	would print from page 5 to the end
pages to print	10 – 15	would print pages 10 to 15 inclusive
pages to print	7,9,22	would print pages 7, 9 and 22 only.

serial storage and access Data is stored on magnetic tape in sequential order, ie the first piece of data is saved at the beginning of the tape, the second piece on the next part and so on. In order to recall this data to the screen the tape must move over the read head until the data required is found. This is also known as sequential storage and access. (See **random access**.)

service codes (trace codes) Symbols displayed on the word processor screen to indicate the presence of commands within the text. These symbols are not printed when a hard copy is produced on the printer. The actual symbols displayed differ, depending on the word processing system used.

Here are some examples of service codes. A ›
soft return may be indicated by an arrow at the ›
end of a line. A hard return may be indicated by ›
a square block.□

An arrow may indicate that text extends →
beyond the screen display at the right hand side. □

On·some·systems·each·hard·space·is·shown·by ›
a·dot·like·this.□

service or trace codes

On some systems all the service codes are displayed permanently on the screen, but on others only the most important codes, such as a hard return, are displayed. Experienced operators do not need to see the codes unless they are trying to trace an error, when they may find the codes helpful. For this reason service codes are sometimes referred to as trace codes.

shared logic In word processing terms, the sharing of a central processing unit and a hard disk store by a number of workstations.

shared resources (shared facilities) On a networked system a number of word processors may share the use of disk storage and a printer or other peripheral device. This is an economical way of using expensive computer equipment that might not be fully used if each workstation were equipped with its own printer, etc.

sheet feeder A paper storage cassette attached to a printer that automatically feeds a single sheet of paper into the correct position in the printer as each page is to be printed. When the printed pages are ejected from the printer they fall into a collection tray where they are stacked until the operator removes them. (See **hopper feed**.)

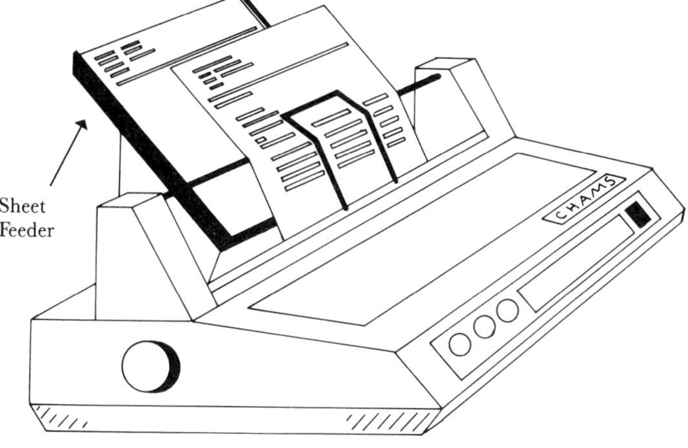

sheet feeder

shift key A key that is depressed so that upper-case (capital) letters can be typed. The shift key is also depressed to type the upper symbol on keys marked with two symbols or with a number and a symbol.

shift lock key The shift lock key is pressed down and automatically locked so that a series of capital letters can be typed. The key remains locked until it is pressed again to release it.

signatory The person who signs a letter or other document.

silicon chip (See **microchip**.)

single line display Some electronic typewriters have a single line, or thin window, on which a limited number of characters are displayed as they are typed. (See **display**.)

skeleton letter A standard letter prepared in such a way that variable information such as the name and address of the recipient, the salutation and details within the letter such as the date of a meeting, may be inserted on a copy of the document. When a typewriter is used to prepare a skeleton letter, spaces are left within the text so that the variable details may be typed in the appropriate positions on a photocopy of the letter.

When a word processor is used, a master skeleton letter is stored on disk and this may be copied and the variable details keyed in at the appropriate insertion points. Alternatively, the skeleton letter may be merged automatically with variable details selected from a data record file. (See **list processing, mail merge, merge** and **standard letter**.)

```
Our ref RJMcK/LPS


*


Dear *

APPLICATION FOR EMPLOYMENT

Thank you for your application for the post of *
with this company.

Will you please attend for interview at * on *,
bringing with you any certificates you may possess.

A map is enclosed showing the location of our
offices, together with details of bus routes that
are suitable if you are travelling by bus.

Please confirm, as soon as possible, that you
intend to be present for this interview.

Yours faithfully
PARKLAND EXHIBITION ORGANISERS


R J McKechnie
PERSONNEL MANAGER


Encs
```

skeleton letter with insertion points for variable details.

soft copy Text displayed on the word processor screen, as compared with hard copy which is text that has been printed out. (See **hard copy**.)

soft hyphen (discretionary hyphen) A hyphen inserted by the word processor to indicate the division of a word at the end of a line as a result of the use of the hyphenation function, as compared with a hard hyphen keyed in by the operator. If the hyphenated word is moved from the end to the middle of a line as a result of editing changes, the soft hyphen will automatically be removed by the system.

soft page break A page break automatically inserted to indicate the end of a page of text, as compared with a hard page break entered by the operator. (See **page break**.)

soft return A return entered by the word processing system at the end of a line of text when the wordwrap or wraparound function is in operation, as compared with the hard return entered by the operator by pressing the return or enter key. If the line endings are changed when editing is carried out, the soft returns are automatically removed and inserted in the appropriate places. (See **hard return**.)

soft space A space automatically inserted between words by a word processor to ensure that each line of text ends at the same point in a justified right margin, as compared with a hard space entered by pressing the space bar. If editing changes are made the system will automatically remove any unnecessary soft spaces to adjust the line length as appropriate. A hard space, on the other hand, can only be removed if the operator deletes it.

software The programs that can be run on a computer, including operating systems and applications packages. (See **applications program**.)

software licence An agreement between the supplier and purchaser of a computer or word processing program describing the user's rights in connection with the software and the copyright restrictions that apply.

software package (See **applications program**.)

sorting The placing of data, such as names and addresses, in a specified order. Items may be sorted into alphabetical, numerical or chronological order (date or time). Within those categories they may be sorted into ascending order, ie A–Z, 1–100, 1990–2001, 0001 hours to 1159 hours, or descending order, ie Z–A, 100–1, 2001–1990, 1159 hours to 0001 hours.

space bar A long key below the bottom row of keys of a QWERTY keyboard which, when pressed, inserts a blank character space.

special directions Notes may be included on an envelope and letter or memo to indicate special directions, such as PERSONAL, PRIVATE, CONFIDENTIAL, FIRST CLASS MAIL or URGENT.

speech recognition The recognition and interpretation by a computer or word processor of a fairly limited range of commands given by means of the spoken word. This method of input is useful if people are unwilling to use the keyboard (eg, non-typing business executives) or are able to do so only with difficulty (eg, disabled people).

speech synthesis The production of a sound corresponding to the spoken word in a more or less human-sounding voice. This may be used on some systems for operator prompts, particularly if the equipment is operated by blind users.

speed Typewriting speed is normally quoted in words typed per minute and calculated on the basis of one word equalling five keystrokes. A keystroke includes depression of a character key or a function key such as the shift key, the space bar or the return key. Typewriting speed is usually measured in timed tests on straightforward printed copy. However, this is a fairly artificial measurement and speed of production is more relevant to an employer. Production speed includes the time taken in reading and interpreting the copy, making decisions, typing, correcting and proofreading.

spelling checker A program, or part of a program, for checking the spelling of a word processed document. The spelling check usually takes place while the document is displayed on the screen. Any word that is likely to contain a spelling mistake is identified or highlighted by the system. Some word processing spelling checkers offer alternative spellings by means of a screen prompt. (See **dictionary**.)

split screen A term used to refer to the division of the screen display of a word processor into separate areas, or *windows*, so that different parts of a document may be viewed, or so that different documents may be viewed simultaneously. The screen may be split horizontally or vertically, depending on the system used. (See **windows**.)

spooler (See **print queue**.)

standalone An independent word processing workstation that includes all the hardware and software necessary for operation, ie visual display unit, central processing unit, disk drives, keyboard and printer. (See page 125.)

standard document A document containing standard information that applies to all recipients, eg, a letter which is to be sent to a number of people inviting them to a special ceremony. A standard document may or may not include spaces for the insertion of variable information.

A standard letter that does include insertion points for variable details may be automatically merged with names and addresses stored in a data record file to produce a personalised letter for each individual. (See **mail merge** and **skeleton letter**.)

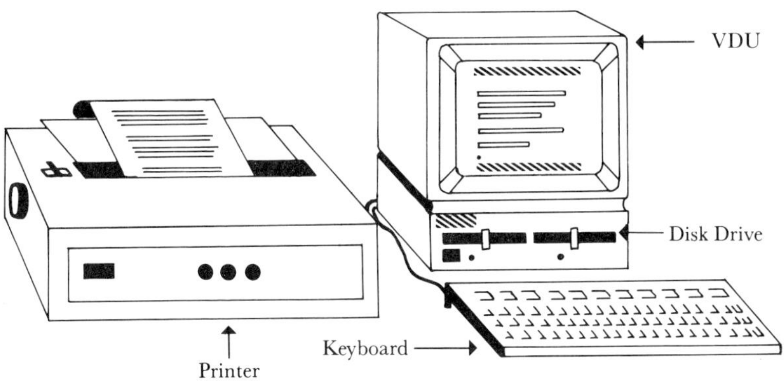

standalone word processor

standard paragraph file A special file in which are stored specially prepared paragraphs that can be selected and merged to form a new document with little or no new keying. (See **boilerplating.**)

CUSTOMER SERVICES DEPARTMENT

STANDARD PARAGRAPH FILE A

(A1) Thank you for your letter concerning the * purchased from one of our BETTABYER stores.

(A2) Thank you for returning the * purchased from one of our BETTABYER stores.

(A3) Our service engineer has examined this carefully and found that there is a fault in the electrical wiring system.

(A4) Our service engineer has examined this carefully and found that there is a mechanical fault in the product.

(A5) Our service engineer has examined this carefully and he assures us that it is in satisfactory working order. May we respectfully suggest that you ensure the power is switched on before using the machine.

(A6) We have therefore despatched a replacement to you today, together with a cheque to cover the costs incurred in returning the product to us.

(A7) We therefore enclose a voucher for a replacement, together with a cheque to cover the costs incurred in returning the product to us. If you take this to your nearest BETTABYER store the manager will be pleased to supply you with a new model.

(A8) We are therefore returning the product to you today under separate cover.

(A9) Please do not hesitate to write to us again if you have any further problems.

standard paragraph file

starting up (See **log on**.)

static electricity A magnetic field existing around most electrical equipment, including the screen of a word processor, which can cause dust particles to be attracted to the screen. Minute electrical shocks can be experienced when touching such equipment, especially if man-made fibres are worn and/or carpeting of man-made fibres is used as floor covering. Static electricity can cause operating problems to computer or word processor systems, and for this reason it is desirable to reduce the incidence of static by using special anti-static carpets.

status line An area of the word processor screen in the form of a narrow band at the top or bottom of the screen on which information is displayed regarding the state of the current document. Typical information displayed on the status line includes the name of the document, the page number of the page currently displayed on the screen, line and column positions of the cursor, line spacing, type size, whether the system is in overtype or insert mode and whether justification is on or off, as shown in the example below.

REPORT	Page 4	Line 22	Col 48	Pitch 12	Mode INSERT	Just'n ON

status line

store and forward A system in electronics communications that passes message packets from one location to another and stores them at intermediate points until the appropriate time to transmit them to their destination. (See **message switching**.)

string A series of characters and/or numbers or symbols that is recognised by the word processor as text. The string may consist of a single character, a word or several words. The term *string* is used on many systems instead of *word* or *words* in the search operation.

A unique string is one that appears only once in the document. If you wish, for example, to search for the words *international sales* but know that these words appear several times in the document, you can search for a unique string by including the words preceding and following that string, eg, *increased international sales this year.*

style sheet A master document containing preset format and layout instructions that can be saved and copied for use on many occasions, thus saving the time that would be spent setting up the appropriate format. This may also be termed a template.

subscript Characters, numbers or symbols printed below the normal line of type, eg, H_2SO_4. Subscript characters are sometimes referred to as inferior characters. The subscript function may also be used if you wish to align one line of type vertically against two or more lines of text, eg:

```
Text occupying )
an even number )
of lines within) Subscripted text
a brace        )
```

superior character (See **superscript**.)

superscript Characters, numbers or symbols printed above the normal line of type, eg, x^2 xy^3 + a^{-10}. Superscript characters are sometimes referred to as superior characters.

system A term frequently used to refer to a word processor or computer, central processing unit, disk drives, keyboard and printer and the appropriate software.

system disk The disk containing the word processing program, as compared with the working disk or data disk containing stored text.

T

tab key (tabulator key) A key that automatically advances the typing point (or cursor) to the next preset tab stop.

tab stop (tabulator stop) A preset position along the typing line. By pressing the tab key the typing point (or cursor) is moved directly to the tab stop instead of tapping the space bar.

Typewriters and word processors will have one or more of the following types of tab stop: normal or left aligned tab, decimal tab, flush right or justified tab and centred tab. Text is aligned in accordance with the tab stop setting used, as shown in the example below:

NORMAL OR LEFT-ALIGNED TAB STOP	DECIMAL TAB STOP	FLUSH RIGHT OR JUSTIFIED TAB STOP	CENTRED TAB STOP
Typewriter	134.57	Folders	Conferences
Computer	99.0412	Pens	Meetings
Telex	1.9	Badges	Talks
Facsimile	172.031	Documents	Displays

tabulation The movement of the typing point (or the cursor) directly to a preset 'stop' position along the line by pressing the tabulator key (tab key).

tailpiece A decorative ending to a document such as a programme, menu or article, formed by using a selection of symbol keys, as shown in the examples below:
(See **decoration**.)

```
*******      -o-o-o-o-o-      ---oOo---      )()()()()(
 *****         -o-o-o-                         )()()(
  ***            -o-                             )(
   *
```

tear-off slip (cut-off slip) A section at the foot of a circular letter or other document that is intended to be completed with appropriate details by the recipient, cut off and returned to the sender. A line is typed across the page from margin to margin using the hyphen key to indicate the point at which the slip should be cut or torn off.

teletext An international electronic mail service. Correspondence prepared on a word processor (or other electronic equipment) is transmitted over the telephone network to a receiving terminal. Teletext is capable of transmitting letters in their normal layout, using both upper- and lower-case letters.

teletex A system for one-way transmission of information in the form of text and graphics from a computer databank. Users can access pages of the *Ceefax* and *Oracle* services provided by the BBC and IBA to view information from the databank on their television sets. (See **videotex**.)

telex An electronic communications system used to send and receive messages over a worldwide network. Transmission speeds are slow in comparison with teletext, and telex can transmit only in upper-case characters. Modern telex terminals have a VDU screen and memory facilities that allow text to be input and edited before transmission.

template (style sheet) A master document set up with a format and layout to suit a particular type of document that is frequently repeated. The master template document is stored on disk so that it can be copied and used whenever necessary, leaving the master document untouched and ready for use again. A number of templates allowing a variety of layouts can be produced and saved under different names.

terminal A term loosely used to describe a workstation connected to a networked computer or word processor installation.

text Any meaningful combination of characters and numbers that conveys information.

text editing The amendment, insertion, deletion, movement, correction and copying of text documents stored on a disk.

text processing (See **word processing**.)

thin window display (See **single line display**.)

tickler file (See **reminder file**.)

time Times of day may be typed in either the 12-hour clock form or the 24-hour clock form. Type 12-hour clock times with a full stop to separate the hours and minutes, eg, *11.30 am*. Note that there are no full stops in the abbreviation *am* when the open punctuation style is used. Alternatively 12-hour clock times may be typed as *4 o'clock*.

Type 24-hour clock times *without* a full stop to separate the hours and minutes, starting at 0001 and continuing to 2399, with the word *hours* typed after the time, eg, *0945 hours* and *1035 hours*.

time management system (See **diary systems**.)

toggle switch A two-position switch that is either in the *on* or *off* position.

touch screen A VDU screen that enables commands to be input to a computer or word processing system by touching the appropriate point. A menu of options may be displayed and the desired option is chosen by touching the screen.

trace codes (See **service codes**.)

track The area on a magnetic disk on which information is stored. A track is one bit wide and forms a complete circle around a disk. There are many tracks on a disk, the circumference of each track becoming smaller as the tracks get nearer to the centre of the disk.

trackball An input device, similar in concept to the mouse except that the small unit housing the rolling ball remains stationary on the desk. The rolling ball is on top of the unit and the user directs the cursor movement in the appropriate direction by moving the ball with the fingertips.

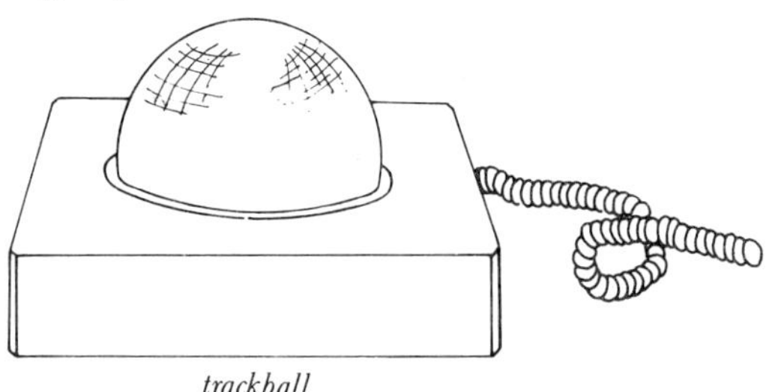

trackball

tractor feed A mechanical device for feeding continuous stationery through a printer. The paper has a continuous strip at each side containing a series of regularly spaced holes. These fit over sprockets (studs) and as the tractor feed mechanism rotates the paper is fed evenly through the printer.

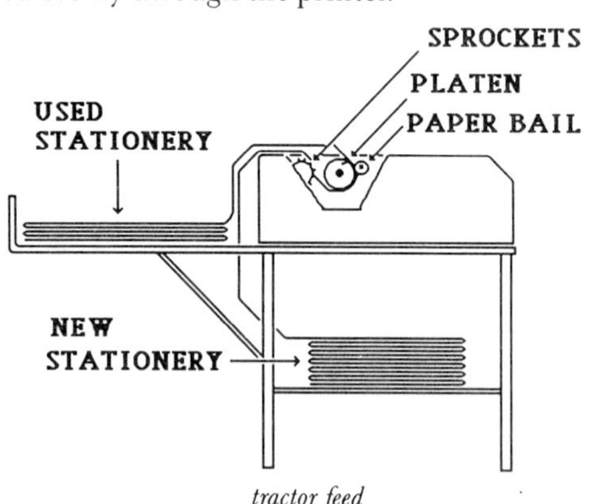

tractor feed

transcription The conversion of dictated information (that has been recorded in shorthand, on an audio tape or in handwriting) into text, using a typewriter or word processor.

transposition Changing the position of words or figures in response to an editing instruction written on the copy by an author, eg:

```
Change the order of these figures and words.

        Ribbons    £5.50 and £7.05
        Disks      £4.50 to £6.25
```

turnaround time The time taken to process a document from despatch to receipt of completed material, including keying in, proofreading and checking, correction where necessary, printing and return to the author.

typeface (See **font**.)

type sizes The size of type on a typewriter is measured in terms of the number of characters that can be typed within the space of one inch (25 mm). The type sizes generally available on typewriters are 10, 12 and 15 characters to the inch. A much wider range of type sizes is available on many word processing systems. (See **pitch** and **print styles**.)

typographical error Any mistake made when typing text, as compared with a layout or formatting error.

U

underline function A word processor function that underlines text. The underline function is used where the underscore key would be used on a typewriter. Many word processors offer various options, including single or double underlining and continuous or separate word underlining.

Sample of underlining	SINGLE CONTINUOUS UNDERLINE
Sample of underlining	SINGLE WORD ONLY UNDERLINE
Sample of underlining	DOUBLE CONTINUOUS UNDERLINE
Sample of underlining	DOUBLE WORD ONLY UNDERLINE

types of underline

underscore A line typed immediately below text by using the underscore key on a typewriter.

undo A useful word processing function that reverses a command that has just been carried out. You may, for example, instruct the word process r to centre a line of text and find you have centred the wrong line. By pressing the undo key, or activating the undo function, the centring will be removed from that line of text. The function will only work immediately after the command has been carried out. If you have pressed any other keys after entering a command the undo function cannot be used.

updating Changing or editing documents so that they comply with current needs. Price lists, for example, may be updated by changing the description or price of an item.

In word processing terms updating means replacing text stored on a disk with a revised version.

upgrade In word processing the term upgrade refers to improving the existing hardware by increasing the memory capacity or adding facilities or peripherals. It is also used to describe the improvement of software such as a word processing program.

upper-case characters (See **capitals**.)

user defined keys (See **keystroke memory**.)

user friendly A term describing a word processing program which has been designed so that it is easy to use with a minimum of operator training and helps the operator to gain the maximum benefit from the system. This is generally accomplished by the use of menus and screen prompts in straightforward English to guide the operator through procedures. Some programs include a 'help' file that can be referred to at any time to reduce the need to refer to the printed manual.

user group Individuals who use a particular program or computer/word processor and who form a group to share information and help each other by corresponding or circulating a newsletter/magazine. Some user groups are large enough to make representations to manufacturers of the program or equipment in question and to pass on the views of users in the hope that improvements may be made.

user manual A book of instructions intended to explain the operation and use of a software program or word processing/computer hardware.

V

variable information Information that changes from one document to another. The term is generally used in connection with standard or circular letters where specific points of the letter are coded so that variable details can be automatically inserted by the word processor. (See **skeleton letter**.)

vertical heading A heading to a column of information that is typed sideways in order to save space. (See **heading**.)

vertical scrolling (See **scrolling**.)

vertical space The white space between or alongside rows of text. Vertical space is measured in terms of line spacing, there being six single lines to one inch.

video conferencing (teleconferencing) A means of holding a meeting between two or more groups of people at different locations that allows the participants to see and hear each other and, for example, view and discuss diagrams and plans. The pictures and sound are transmitted by telecommunications networks and satellites. Video conferencing saves time and money and allows people to be called into the room who might not otherwise have been present if both groups had met at one particular site.

video display Any electronic screen on which text or graphics can be displayed. It may be a cathode-ray tube, a light-emitting diode (LED) or a plasma panel.

videotex The international term used to describe viewdata and teletex services that display on a screen information accessed from a central databank. (See **teletex** and **viewdata**.)

viewdata An information service connecting subscribers with a central computer by means of a telephone network and allowing access to information stored in databanks. The information is displayed on the screen of a word processor or computer, or on a television set fitted with a special adaptor.

Viewdata systems are interactive, which means they are two-way systems, allowing the user to send messages as well as receive information (unlike teletex, which is a receive-only information service). A user may, for example, view a page advertising goods for sale and then transmit an order using the keypad connected to the terminal.

British Telecom's public viewdata service is known as Prestel. Subscribers to this service may view certain pages free of charge or pay to access other pages of information. A large number of private viewdata systems are available only to specific groups of people, such as travel agents, stockbrokers or motor vehicle distributors. Many organisations have set up their own in-house viewdata services that provide information and response facilities for members of staff. (See **videotex**.)

visual display unit (VDU) The part of a word processor that houses the screen.

voice input (voice recognition) Some systems can be 'trained' to recognise a user's voice and to respond to it. Short, clearly spoken commands can be given to the system such as *print* or *menu* and the system will print a document or display a menu.

W

waste bin A memory area in some word processors to which unwanted documents are consigned prior to permanent deletion. As long as they remain in the waste bin they can be retrieved, but once the system has been switched off the documents are deleted permanently.

wide area network (WAN) A communications network system connecting large numbers of terminals spread over a wide area. A wide area network may incorporate one or more local area networks, and is capable of longer-distance communications than a local area network. (See **local area network**.)

wide document Any document wider than the screen display. Although most word processing systems display 80 characters across the screen, it is possible to prepare documents wider than this. The screen display scrolls to the left as a long line of text is typed and returns to the left margin position for the start of the next line. Horizontal scrolling is used to proofread the document on the screen. Before printing, ensure that the printer is set up for printing a wide document and that the stationery is fed into the printer in the appropriate position.

widow line The first line of a paragraph of text is called a widow when it is separated from the rest of the paragraph by a page break, ie the first line is printed at the bottom of one page and the rest of the paragraph is printed at the top of the next page. This is undesirable in layout terms, and the page length should be adjusted so that the single line is taken on to the next page. (See **orphan line**.)

Winchester disk drive A sealed hard disk unit with high performance speeds and high storage capacity. Sizes currently available include 5.25 inches, 8 inches and 14 inches.

window A rectangular area on a word processor screen in which a document can be displayed. More than one window can be displayed at once so that a number of documents can be viewed at the same time. Text can be cut or copied from one document and moved to a document in another window. (See **split screen**.) (See page 137.)

window envelope An envelope that incorporates a rectangle of transparent material in the position where the address is normally typed. The letter is folded so that when it is inserted into the envelope the addressee details typed on the letter can be seen through the window, thereby eliminating the need to type the address on the envelope.

A similar type of envelope incorporates a cut away rectangle that is not covered with transparent material, and this is known as an aperture envelope.

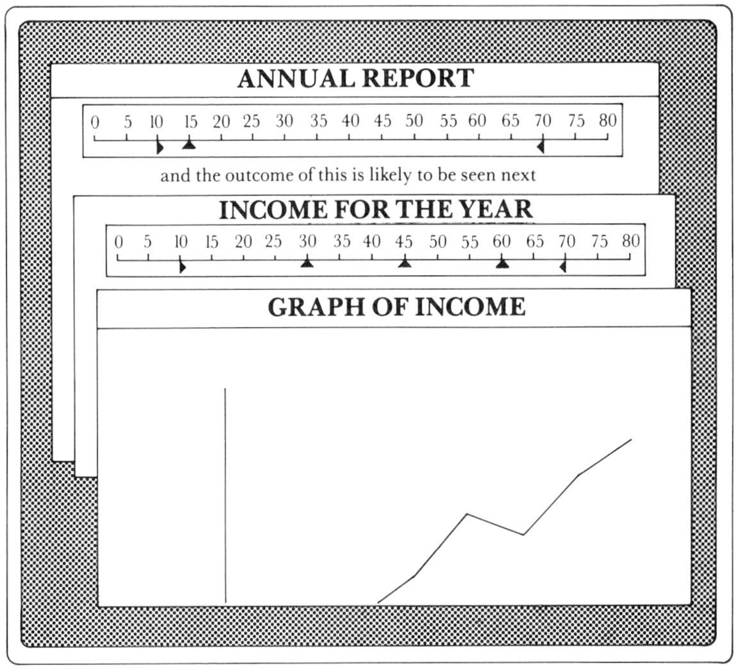

windows

word In word processing terms a word is any character or series of characters with a space each side. In the measurement of typewriting speed a word is considered as five keystrokes, including characters and spaces. (See **speed**.)

word processing The use of a word processor for preparation, printing, storage and editing of documents.

word processor A typical word processing system consists of a visual display unit, a central processing unit, a disk drive, a keyboard and a printer. A dedicated system is a computer designed and used solely for word processing operations. Many individuals and organisations use a word processing program on a microcomputer, which provides the user with the facility for running other applications programs such as spreadsheets and databases.

A number of workstations may be linked in the form of a network to enable operators to share resources such as printers. Word processing facilities may also be provided for users of minicomputers and mainframe computers.

The number of advanced features available on word processors varies from program to program, as does the ease with which the functions and operations can be carried out.

wordwrap (See **wraparound**.)

working disk (data disk) The disk to which your work is saved when word processing, as compared with the system disk which contains the word processing program.

workstation A term used loosely to describe a word processor or computer and the operator's working area.

wraparound (wordwrap) The ability of a word processor to assess automatically the amount of text that can be fitted on to a line and to take the next word down to the following line without the need for the operator to press the return key.

When editing operations are carried out on existing text the wraparound function will automatically readjust the lines of text. This is also known as wordwrap.

write protection A method of preventing anyone from accidentally overwriting files or documents stored on a disk. On a floppy disk a self-adhesive label is stuck over the write-enable notch. On a microfloppy disk a small square of plastic is slid from the write enable position to the write protect position. This prevents the drive head from writing data to the disk. If necessary, the label, etc, may be removed so that documents may be edited.

writing to disk The process of saving text on to a working disk.

WYSIWYG An abbreviation for What You See Is What You Get, pronounced 'wizzywig'. This indicates that a word processing system displays text on the screen exactly as it will look when it is printed out, showing the line spacing, underlining, emboldening, centring and in some cases even the font and type size that have been selected.

Z

zap A term used on used some word processors to refer to the deletion of text or of a document.

ABBREVIATIONS

A

abbr, abbrev	abbreviation
ab init	from the beginning (*ab initio*)
abs, absol	absolute(ly)
abt	about
A/C, a/c	account
ACAS	Advisory, Conciliation and Arbitration Service
accom	accommodation
acct	accountant
ack	acknowledge
AD	in the year of the Lord (*anno Domini*)
ad, advt, advert	advertisement
admin	administration
AGM, agm	annual general meeting
AHA	Area Health Authority
am	before noon (*ante meridiem*)
amt	amount
anon	anonymous(ly)
ans	answer
AOB, aob	any other business
appro	approval
approx	approximately
appt	appointment
APR	annual percentage rate
Apr	April
arr	arrive, arrival
arrge	arrange
asap	as soon as possible
ASCII	American Standard Code for Information Interchange
ass, assoc, assn	association
asst	assistant
AST	Atlantic Standard Time
att	attached, attachment
attrib	attribute(d)
Aug	August
auto	automatic(ally)

AV	audio-visual
av, avge	average
ave	avenue

B

BACS	Bankers' Automated Clearing Service
bal	balance
BASIC	Beginner's All-purpose Symbolic Instruction Code
BC	before Christ
B/E	bill of exchange
Beds	Bedfordshire
bel	believe
Berks	Berkshire
bet	between
bf, b/f	brought forward
B/ham	Birmingham
biog	biography
BIT	Binary Digit
bk	book, bank
bkg	banking
B/L	bill of lading
bldg	building
Blvd, Boul	Boulevard
BSI	British Standards Institute
BST	British Summer Time, British Standard Time
Bucks	Buckinghamshire
bus	business

C

°C	degree(s) Celcius
©	copyright
ca	about (*circa*)
Cam, Camb	Cambridge
Cambs	Cambridgeshire
Cant	Canterbury
cap	capital
caps	capitals
cat	catalogue
cc	carbon copy, cubic centimetre(s)
c/d	carried down
cen	central, century
cert	certificate, certainty
chron	chronological
circs	circumstances

Cl	Close
cl	centilitre(s)
cm	centimetre(s)
co	company
c/o	care of
COD	cash on delivery
col	column
com	commerce
COM	computer output on microfilm
commn	commission, communication
conn	connection, connected
cont, contd	continued
co-op	co-operative
corr	correspond, correspondence
coy	company
cp	carriage paid
cpi	characters per inch
cps	characters per second
CPU	central processing unit
cr	credit, creditor
Cres, Cresc	Crescent
CRT	cathode ray tube
C/T	credit transfer
ct	carat
cttee	committee
cu	cubic
cur	current
CV	curriculum vitae
cwo	cash with order
cwt	hundred-weight

D

3-D	three dimensional
DATEC	data and telecommunications
dB	decibel
DBMS	database management system
dd	direct debit
Dec	December
dec	deceased
def	definite, definition
deg	degree(s)
del	delete, delegate
dep	depart(s), departure, deputy
dept	department
Derbys	Derbyshire

dev develop
devpt development
dg decigram(s)
diam diameter
dict dictionary
diff different, difference
dis discontinued
disc discount
dist distance, district
div divide, dividend
divn division
DIY do-it-yourself
dl decilitre(s)
dm decimetre(s)
do the same (*ditto*)
dob date of birth
DOS disk operating system
doz dozen
DP data processing
Dr Doctor, Drive
dr dear, dram
DT data transmission
DTP desktop publishing

E
E Sussex East Sussex
E&OE errors and omissions excepted
eaon except as otherwise noted
ECU European currency unit
Ed Editor
Edin Edinburgh
EET Eastern European Time
EFT electronic funds transfer
EFTPOS electronic funds transfer at point of sale
eg for example (*exempli gratia*)
elec, elect electric, electricity
E-mail electronic mail
EMF European Monetary Fund
EMS European Monetary System
emu electromagnetic unit
enc(s) enclosure(s)
Eng England, English
EOC Equal Opportunities Commission
EPROM erasable programmable read-only memory
esp especially

Esq	Esquire
EST	Eastern Standard Time
est	established, estimated
ETA	estimated time of arrival
et al	and others (*et alii*)
etc, &c	and the others, and so forth (*et ceteri* or *et cetera*)
ETD	estimated time of departure
et seq	and the following (*et sequens*)
ex	examined, example, exception, executive, exercise, export
exc	except, exception
ex officio	by virtue of his office
exp	expense, experience, export
ext	extension, externally, extra, extract

F

°F	degrees Fahrenheit
fam	familiar, family
FAX	facsimile
Feb	February
ffly	faithfully
FIFO	first in, first out
fig	figure
fl oz	fluid ounce
foc	free of charge
Fri	Friday
ft	foot, feet

G

g	gram
gall	gallon
Gdns	Gardens
gen	general
gent	gentleman
GIGO	garbage in, garbage out
Glos	Gloucestershire
gm	gram
GMT	Greenwich Mean Time
gntee	guarantee
gov, govt	government

H

h, hr	hour
ha	hectare
Hants	Hampshire
Herts	Hertfordshire

HGV	heavy goods vehicle
hl	hectolitre(s)
HMSO	Her Majesty's Stationery Office
ho	house
Hon	honorable, honorary
Hon Sec	Honorary Secretary
HP	hire purchase
HQ	headquarters
hr(s)	hour(s)
HSE	Health and Safety Executive
Humb	Humberside
Hz	Hertz

I

ib, ibid	in the same place (*ibidem*)
i/c	in charge
id	the same (*idem*)
ie	that is (*id est*)
ill	illustrated
immed	immediate (ly)
in	inch(es)
inc	including, incorporated
incl	including, included
incon	inconvenient, inconvenience
indef	indefinite
indiv	individual
infra dig	beneath one's dignity (*infra dignitatum*)
inst	instant, institute
instn	institution
int	interest, international
intro	introduction, introductory
IOM	Isle of Man
IOU	I owe you
IOW	Isle of Wight
IP	information processing
IPSS	international packet switchstream
ISBN	International Standard Book Number
ISD	international subscriber dialling
ISO	International Organisation for Standardisation
IT	information technology
ital	italic

J

j	joule
Jan	January
JP	Justice of the Peace

Jr, Jun, Jnr	Junior
Jul	July
Jun	June, junior
junc, junct	junction

K

k	kilo- (1000, or 1024 in computer storage locations)
kb	kilobyte
kg	kilogram
kilo	kilogram, kilometre
km	kilometre
kph	kilometres per hour
kV	kilovolt
kW	kilowatt
kWh	kilowatt-hour

L

l	litre
lab	laboratory
LAN	local area network
Lancs	Lancashire
lang	language
LASER	Light Amplification by Stimulated Emission of Radiation
lat	latitude
lb	pound (weight) (*libra*)
lc	lower-case
LCCI	London Chamber of Commerce and Industry
LCD	liquid crystal display
LED	light-emitting diode
Leics	Leicestershire
lh	left-hand
Lincs	Lincolnshire
Lond	London
lpm	lines per minute
L/pool	Liverpool
Ltd	limited liability

M

Mar	March
max	maximum
m/c	machine
M/cr	Manchester
Mddx	Middlesex
m/f	more follows

mfr, mnfr	manufacturer
mgr	manager
MICR	magnetic ink character recognition
Mid Glam	Mid Glamorgan
Min	Ministry
min	minimum, minute
misc	miscellaneous
ml	millilitre(s)
mm	millimetre(s)
mo	month
mod	modern
mod con	modern convenience
modem	modulator-demodulator
Mon	Monday
MP	Member of Parliament
mpg	miles per gallon
mph	miles per hour
ms	millisecond(s)
ms(s)	manuscript(s)
mth	month
mts	mountains
mus	museum

N

N	Newton, north, northern
NB	note well, or take notice
NCR	no carbon required
ncv	no commercial value
NEC	National Exhibition Centre (Birmingham)
nec, necy	necessary
neg	negative
nem con	no-one contradicting (*nemine contradicente*)
nem diss	no-one dissenting (*nemine dissentiente*)
N/F	no funds
NI	Northern Ireland, national insurance
nop	not otherwise provided
Northants	Northamptonshire
Notts	Nottinghamshire
Nov	November
NP, np	new paragraph
nr	near
nvd	no value declared

O

o/a	on account of
O&M	organisation and method

o/c	overcharge
OCR	optical character recognition
Oct	October
O/D	overdrawn
off	official
ono	or nearest offer
opp	opportunity, opposite
ord	ordinary
orig	original(ly)
O/S	outstanding
oz	ounce(s)

P

P&P	postage and packing
PA	personal assistant, public address (system)
pa	per annum
PABX	private automatic branch exchange
para	paragraph
PAYE	pay as you earn
pc	postcard, per cent
pce	piece
pd	paid
per pro	by the agency (of) (*per procurationem*)
pm	afternoon (*post meridiem*)
po	postal order
POD	pay on delivery
pop	popular, population
POP	post office preferred
pp	pages
pr	pair
prep	preparation
pro	professional
Prof	Professor
PROM	programmable read-only memory
prop	properly, property
pro tem	for the time being (*pro tempore*)
PSS	packet switchstream
PSTN	public switched telephone network
PTO	please turn over

Q

qv	which see (*quod vide*)

R

RAM	random access memory

R & D	research and development
Rd	Road
re	with reference to, with regard to
rec	receipt, receive
recd	received
recom	recommend
ref	referee, reference
refd	referred
reg, regd	registered
rep	representative, report
resp	responsible
rh	right-hand
rly	railway
ROM	read-only memory
Ro-Ro	roll on, roll off
rpm	revolutions per minute
RSA	Royal Society of Arts
RSVP	please reply (*répondez s'il vous plaît*)

S

S Yorks	South Yorkshire
sae	stamped addressed envelope
Salop	Shropshire
Sat	Saturday
SAYE	save as you earn
s/c	self-contained
sec, secy	secretary
Sen	Senior
sep	separate
Sep, Sept	September
sh	shall
shd	should
SI	Système International (d'Unités)
sic	so written
sig	signature
soc, socy	society
sol, solr	solicitor
Sr	senior
ssly	sincerely
St	Street
Staffs	Staffordshire
STD	subscriber trunk dialling
std	standard
stet	let it stand
stg	sterling
subs	substitute, sub-standard

suff	sufficient
Sun	Sunday
supp	supplement, supplementary

T

t	tonne
tel	telephone
temp	temperature, temporary
Terr	Terrace
th	that
tho	though
thro', thru	through
Thur, Thurs	Thursday
tr, trs	transpose
Tue, Tues	Tuesday
TV	television
typo	typographical (error)

U

uc	upper-case
UHF	ultra high frequency
UK	United Kingdom
UN	United Nations
US	United States

V

v	versus
vac	vacation
val	value
VAT	value added tax
VDT	video display terminal
VDU	visual display unit
VHF	very high frequency
via	by way of
VIP	very important person
viz	namely (*videlicet*)
vol	volume

W

W	watt
w	with
W Glam	West Glamorgan
W Mids	West Midlands
W Sussex	West Sussex

W Yorks	West Yorkshire
WAN	wide area network
W/B	week beginning
wd	would
W/E	week ending
Wed, Weds	Wednesday
wef	with effect from
wh	which
Wilts	Wiltshire
WIMP	window, icon, mouse, pointer
wk	week
wl	will
Worcs	Worcestershire
WORM	write once, read many (times)
WP	word processing, word processor
wpb	waste paper basket
wpm	words per minute
WYSIWYG	what you see is what you get

X

Xmas	Christmas

Y

y	yard, year
yd	yard
Yorks	Yorkshire
yr	year, your

Z

ZST	Zone Standard Time

Chambers Commerce Series

Keyboarding

A Universal Approach to Basic Typewriting Skills

Derek Stananought

Keyboarding provides a clear approach to the acquisition of skills in using manual typewriters, electric and electronic typewriters, word processors or computers. The book includes background information related to 'new technology' and the electronic office. A variety of exercise material is included, covering basic keyboarding instruction, proof reading, speed development, practical application of typing skills, and 'Test Your Knowledge' sections.

0 550 20705 8